EVERYMAN'S LIBRARY
EDITED BY ERNEST RHYS

ESSAYS AND
BELLES LETTRES

THE CROWN OF WILD
OLIVE, ETC. WITH INTRODUC-
TION BY CLIFFORD BAX

1908.

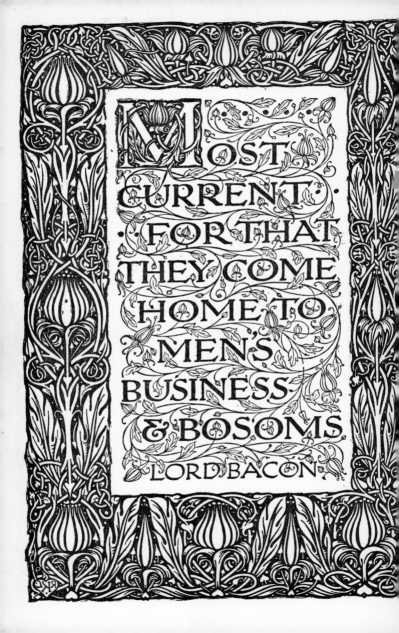

MOST CURRENT FOR THAT THEY COME HOME TO MEN'S BUSINESS & BOSOMS

LORD BACON

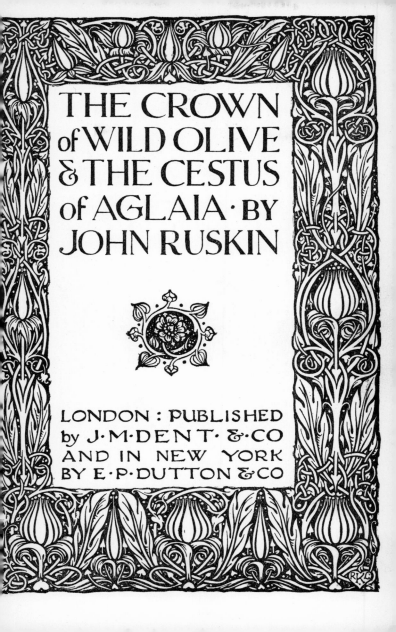

THE CROWN of WILD OLIVE & THE CESTUS of AGLAIA · BY JOHN RUSKIN

LONDON : PUBLISHED by J · M · DENT · & CO AND IN NEW YORK BY E · P · DUTTON & CO

INTRODUCTION

ALREADY to idealists of the younger generation the sombre years in which Ruskin wrote have begun to be touched with beauty, and even with romance. The imagination delights to inhabit, as far as it may, that era when the great poets were building up the Elizabethan drama, and now we begin to recall, almost in the same way, the period when Rossetti, Morris, and Burne-Jones were creating in the least romantic of ages the most romantic of all poems or paintings in the story of English art.

Much of their earliest impulse was due to the influence of Ruskin, and all through the time when they were painting and writing he was labouring to evoke, in the English people, a reverence for beauty and a more intelligent religious interest in art. He was never wearied of demonstrating the high position which ought to be given to the arts in the life of a civilised people, for he knew that when a nation adds nothing to the beauty of the world, it is remembered neither clearly nor with affection by the men of after-times. And as we read the lectures in this book it is not easy to realise that their author is no more living, so real and so passionately felt are the words that were spoken half a century ago. Nor in truth for any but those who " make their dullard's distinction between life and books " is Ruskin an influence of the past. His words are the living reflection of a spirit beautiful and fearless. Every page still burns with an unrelenting sincerity, and we cannot put aside the truth if it disturbs us by the assurance that the writer really cares but little for what he declares. Ruskin did not fear to strike boldly at the rotten roots of a nation, and he took up his position without any thought of escape. To do this great courage was needed, since such work immediately provokes conservative criticism and the resistance of those who only live by tradition.

The root-quality of Ruskin's nature was a profound admiration for order; it was this that led him to seek out and enunciate broad principles or theories whether in ethics or in art. In the statement of these principles he often displays a striking dramatic sense. His lectures open with some astonishing statement which holds fast the attention by rousing that feeling of suspense which is the secret of dramatic effect. When he addresses an audience of young soldiers, he wins their attention at the outset by declaring that in a warless nation the arts inevitably wane! Under the imminence of war men live intensely, he tells them, and this quickening of energy, being magnetic, imparts a new virility to craftsmen and thinkers, and kindles a fresh fire. It is only when thus he has won their sympathy that he qualifies the statement and shows his audience that the soldiers' duty is not merely to obey, but to obey the right, and that war which is wrongly undertaken can never have any beneficial result. Perhaps no better illustration of this dramatic treatment may be found than in the famous lecture in *The Two Paths* where he compares the elaborate art of India with the artlessness of Scotland, for the comparison threatens to destroy utterly the principle which opens the discourse. He delights in this way to confront himself with difficulties, and to go forth to battle with Goliath.

But apart from the method of his argument, and the rightness or wrongness of his thought, there is here, as in every one of Ruskin's books, the particular element of his style to be considered. Lecturing or writing, he spoke or wrote when he was most inspired, with a faultless ear for music, and with a strength, a suppleness and a variety that are lacking in the pages of the greatest of his contemporaries. Two among them have especially

been compared with him: Walter Pater and Matthew
Arnold. But Pater's style remains monotonous because it lies unchangingly at the same level, or it is too
bewilderingly ornate; and Arnold's style, while it has
a classic power, lacks that rarer grace of prose when
a thought like a dancer moves apparently careless but
really lost in her own delight. The style of Walter
Pater, though too minutely stippled, is that of a great
artist in words; Matthew Arnold wrote as an architect
may build. But the style of John Ruskin is that of a
poet before whom words are obedient, who moulds them
entirely at will to shapes of lightness or of strength,
illuminating the scheme of the builder with glowing
colour.

Yet fervour of feeling and beauty of phrase can hardly
of itself give greatness to poetry or prose; for this the
architectural element, the subservience of the parts to
the whole, a sacrifice from which they gain so much, is
fundamentally needed, and Ruskin (perhaps on account
of his long and profound study of architecture) possessed
in a large measure the sense of unity and structure. In
the lecture on " Traffic " he speaks of the three great
European styles, the Grecian, the Gothic and the
Renaissance, remarking of the second how it is " conceived in a mingled sentiment of melancholy and aspiration, partly severe, partly luxuriant, which will lend
itself to every one of our needs and every one of our
fancies." " Partly severe, partly luxuriant " are words
that apply well to his own style, and of this the Introduction to the *Crown of Wild Olive* affords a fine example.

It may be that his ear was too often caught by the
trick of antithesis, and sometimes there is a tendency to
play with words of a similar sound in a manner that
reminds us of the serious puns which mar certain
passages of Egyptian poetry. But these are insignifi-
cant blemishes. In an essay elsewhere he speaks of the
disappointment he felt when the beauty of his expression was praised and the meaning behind it either

ignored or rejected, for as he continually asserted, "the life is more than the meat and the body than the raiment."

There is at present a curious reaction against Ruskin. It is due to several causes, but firstly it falls to the lot of every writer who has won a general acceptance during his lifetime that when he dies he should be largely and suddenly forsaken. In the ten years that follow the death of a prominent man his achievements undergo the severest of all criticism. People imagine that the works he has left must somehow have lost a portion at least of their original life. The new generation is eager for new influences, for something that is not yet finished, that possesses the magnetism of all expanding things. There is the sense of uncertainty, of suspense, which appeals irresistibly to those who are dazzled by the present. To most men the living hour seems ever more weighty and more real than the past, and it is few indeed—only those that are dreaming of the future and are overshadowed by the sense of eternity—who can realise the transience of their own time, regarding the present excitement as they regard the struggles of ended lives.

And thus it is that a writer who has addressed himself to his contemporaries inevitably passes through a period of neglect. He is too complete for the curious multitude and at the same time he is too modern to secure the attention of the studious few. Such is the momentary position of Ruskin. There was an impatience, apparently childish, in some of his utterances, and at certain times he followed his thoughts to the point of exaggeration. It is these qualities, and an unhesitating assurance, which appear to repulse a large number of people who have not gone far enough to discern the grandeur of his main structure. Objections of such a kind are unworthy of consideration; but the main contemporary distrust of Ruskin as a guide would seem to be due to a larger cause. Throughout his life he in-

sisted that the highest art is the outcome of good
thought, and even, in one passage, declares that the
deficiences or defects of certain painters can be detected
in the style of their pictures. He was interested not
only in the fineness of perception and the skill of hand
exhibited in a painting, but quite equally in the quality
of the chosen theme. The little schools of the hour disdain the consideration of subject-matter, and cry with
much insistence that beauty of expression alone can
constitute the artistic value of poem or picture. Beauty
of art, they repeat with much vehemence, need have
no connection with beauty of life and loftiness of aim.
To-day, and ever since the powerful influence of Rossetti
was first felt, the artist has taken the place of the poet.
We read that any mood which has existed has therefore
won the right of artistic embodiment. Perhaps this is
true, but unless the mood have something of aspiration
and nobility it cannot be genuine poetry. There are
those who seek for beauty of treatment and ignore the
selection of theme: others who appreciate poem or
picture regardless of inadequate workmanship, only
caring for the mood or thought beyond it. Both are
at fault, for the latter prove themselves to be void
of a sense for art, and the former of a sense for poetry.
The pure artist has nothing to express but his own perception of beauty; the poet has in addition to this the
whole range of pity, and wonder, tragedy, worship and
joy. The true poet will never be limited by national
and impermanent standards of right and wrong, but
will glory to bind himself by his own perception or instinct of what is noble and what is base. Art is in
truth unmoral; poetry is the loftiest morality of man.

Now, this is assuredly what Ruskin means when
he says in the lecture on " Traffic "—" Tell me what
you like and I'll tell you what you are," for " taste is
the only morality." Art, he declares, ought to lead
men to love and desire the good, and when the good is
discerned as the beautiful and joyous, as it is in the

poetry of Shelley, how swiftly and with what ardour do
we also desire and believe it! The repression of what
is unworthy forms but the basis for spiritual beauty.
The spirit of man destroys, but it also creates and never
destroys the old so completely as when it creates the
new. The soul flies up to a fresh ideal and the earth of
itself recedes.

The same desire for harmony and order permeates the
whole of Ruskin's thought. He knew that beauty is
energy controlled, he felt that the principles of art are
exactly applicable to the conduct of life. In the paper
on " Work," when he makes but two classes of all men,
the workers and the idlers, we find him teaching what is
closely allied to Socialism. But his ideals are touched
with a sense of moral beauty that few practical Social-
ists have included in their systems. In all this part of
his work he shows his kinship with William Morris;
both divine the value of art in a movement that seeks
to unchain the multitude. For it is art which can best
refine and restrain a people that is brought to sudden
freedom, and that would otherwise threaten to demolish
all culture in adapting the world to their sensual and
selfish aims. But Ruskin evolved his own economic
system, and having some intuition of " what thing
cometh after death," was able to root his reforms in the
spiritual nature of man. He believed in the goodness
of humankind; he believed that men would quickly
respond if their duty were made clear and they themselves no longer enslaved by circumstance. " Work,"
he says, " must be honest, useful, and cheerful," and all
that is done without joy can only be thought of as toil.
In these three fathomless words, and the phrase " all
evil is traceable to wealth," he has epitomised his
economic philosophy. Charity, he declares, ought
hardly to exist; for if men were just there would be no
place for charity. And again in *The Cestus of Aglaia*,
those papers that gave an inestimable value to the old
Art Journals of 1865 and 1866, we discern how deeply

he desired that all activities might combine in one great
social harmony. There again he states emphatically
that the aim of art is more than to amuse, and that art
is only justified when it is of service to the best in man,
when beauty of form is given to beauty of thought
alone.

There are men so " practical " that in art they can see
no social value, but Ruskin sought continually to establish the position of art in the scheme of life. He showed
how in art the nations have written, unconsciously
perhaps, their spiritual histories. But so fierce has
become the struggle of man with man, so nearly has
national consciousness become obliterated, that artists
of to-day are driven more and more to take refuge in
themselves, and all but they have so far lost the desire
for beauty that they cannot associate themselves any
longer with the spirit of their age. Art has become
individual, for national aspirations are not now worthy
of expression in sculpture, picture, or poem. Ruskin
saw this clearly and laboured unflaggingly to awaken, in
a larger number of people, some social and moral ideal
that might be fair enough to kindle the praise of the
artist, and in this way remain imperishably recorded.

In latter life he devoted himself especially to the
rousing of a demand for art rather than to a stimulation
of the supply. The intricacies of art in which he had
so deep an interest he designated " trifles," for he felt
perhaps that until the tyranny of relentless toil be
lifted from " misery's multitude," it is vain to hope for
a national aspiration to beauty. There would seem to
be two reasons why the social ideals that he taught
have not yet received an enthusiastic support. In the
first place his life, as he admits, was to some degree
" sheltered," and he did not perhaps quite realise the
complexity of the world. Sometimes, indeed, from
this very simplicity, he seems to approach mere senti-
mentality as when in this book he speaks of the necessity
for men to become as little children. He wished them

to be gentle as doves, but hardly saw the necessity for the serpent's wisdom.

People therefore imagine that the principles he preaches are inapplicable to a busy and unmeditative life. It certainly seems likely that had Ruskin lived more in the world of action he would have modified many of his more exaggerated statements, but in their main tendency he would assuredly have left them as they stand; for in him aspiration was unquenchable.

The real cause of his neglect, we conclude, lies in his greatness. Most men are born with a spiritual inertness, a bias in the direction of the average; they find no joy in the culture of the will, which, after love, is the noblest principle of the soul; they weave the subtlest of all possible excuses for the refusal of a great ideal, for they know that if they should accept it there must follow an entire transformation of the self. Of this they are afraid, for between the new day and the old there is night and a period of solitude, and they do not remember that " the soul is its own refuge and its own witness." A glimpse of the ideal which Ruskin held may be found in the majestic and peerless passage which at the end of the second lecture he quotes from Plato. His dream was largely influenced by the best of mediæval chivalry, which in its turn has been said to have risen from Plato's doctrine of love. In the days to come when " the world is a water at rest," and the heart of man shall have grown to wisdom, surely the figure of Ruskin will shine with something of a seer's glory, and the men of those days will marvel perhaps that one so powerful was able to achieve so little. But he really achieved more than appears on the surface, seeing that he spoke only to the highest nature of men. " For they must be told that they possess at all times, as a gift from the gods, a divine gold and silver in the soul, and have no need of the human."

CLIFFORD BAX.

May 1908.

The following is a list of Ruskin's published works:—

Ruskin's first printed writings were contributions to the " Magazine of Natural History," 1834-6, and poems in " Friendship's Offering," 1835, Oxford prize poem, " Salsette and Elephanta," 1839.

" Modern Painters," Vol. I. 1843; 2nd ed., 1844; 3rd ed., 1846—later ones followed; Vol. II., 1846; Vol. III., 1856; Vol. IV., 1856; Vol. V., 1860. Selections from " Modern Painters " have been published under the titles of " Frondes Agrestes," 1875; " In Montibus Sanctis," 1884; " Coeli Enarrant," 1885.

" Seven Lamps of Architecture," 1849; second edition, 1855. " The Scythian Guest," 1849 (from " Friendship's Offering ") ; " Poems," 1850 (from " Friendship's Offering," " Amaranth," " London Monthly Miscellany," " Keepsake," Heath's " Book of Beauty," with others not previously printed). " Stones of Venice," Vol. I., 1851; second edition, 1858; Vol. II., 1853; second edition, 1867; Vol. III., 1853; second edition, 1867. " The King of the Golden River," 1851; " Notes on the Construction of Sheepfolds," 1851; " Examples of the Architecture of Venice," 1851; " Pre-Raphaelitism," 1851; " The National Gallery," 1852; " Giotto and his works in Padua," 3 parts, 1853, 1854, 1860; " Lectures on Architecture and Painting," 1854, 1855; " The Opening of the Crystal Palace," 1854; Pamphlet for the preservation of Ancient Buildings and Landmarks, 1854; " Notes on the Royal Academy," No. I., 1855 (three editions); No. II., 1856 (six editions); No. III. (four editions), 1857 (two editions); Nos. IV., V. and VI., 1858, 1859, 1875; " The Harbours of England," 1856, 1857, 1859; " Notes on the Turner Gallery at Marlborough House," 1856-7 (several editions in 1857); " Catalogue of the Turner Sketches in the National Gallery," 1857 (two editions); " Catalogue of Turner's Drawings," 1857-8; " The Elements of Drawing," 1857 (two editions); " The Political Economy of Art," 1857, published in 1880 as " A Joy for Ever "; " Inaugural Addresses at the Cambridge School of Art," 1858; " The Geology of Chamouni," 1858; " The Oxford Museum," 1859; " The Unity of Art," 1859; " The Two Paths," 1859; " Elements of Perspective," 1859; " Tree Twigs," 1861; " Catalogue of Turner Drawings presented to the Fitzwilliam Museum," 1861; " Unto this Last," 1862 (from the " Cornhill Magazine "); " Forms of the Stratified Alps of Savoy," 1863; " Of Queen's Gardens," 1864; " Sesame and Lilies," 1865 (two editions); " The Ethics of the Dust," 1866; " The Crown of Wild Olive," 1866 (two editions); " War," 1866; " Time and Tide," 1867; " Leoni, a legend of Italy," 1868 (from " Friendship's Offering "); " Notes on the Employment of the Destitute and Criminal Classes," 1868; " References to Paintings in illustration of Flamboyant Architecture," 1869; " The Mystery of Life and its Arts " (afternoon lectures), 1869; " The Queen of the Air," 1869 (two editions); " The Future of Engand," 1870; " Samuel Prout," 1870 (from " The Art Journal "); " Verona and its Rivers," 1870; " Lectures on Art," 1870; " Drawings and Photographs illustrative of the Architecture of Verona," 1870; " Fors Clavigera," 1871-84;

"Munera Pulveris," 1872; "Aratra Pentelici," 1872; "Instruc-
tions in Elementary Drawing," 1872; "The Relation between
Michael Angelo and Tintoret," 1872; "The Eagle's Nest," 1872;
"Monuments of the Cavalli Family," 1872; "The Nature and
Authority of Miracle" (from the "Contemporary Review"), 1873;
"Val D'Arno," 1874; "Mornings in Florence" (in parts), 1875-7;
"Proserpina" (in parts), 1875-86; Vol. I., 1879; "Deucalion"
(in parts), 1875-83; Vol. I., 1879; Vol. II. (two parts only), 1880,
1883; "Ariadne Florentina," 1876; "Letters to the 'Times' on
Pre-Raphaelite Pictures in the Exhibition of 1854," 1876; "Yew-
dale and its Streamlets," 1877; "St. Mark's Rest" (3 parts),
1877-9, 1884; "Guide to Pictures in the Academy of Arts, Venice,"
1877; "Notes on the Turner Exhibition," 1878; "The Laws of
Fésole" (four parts, 1877-8), 1879; "Notes on the Prout and Hunt
Exhibition," 1879-80; "Circular respecting the Memorial Studies
at St. Mark's," 1879-80; "Letters to the Clergy" (Lord's Prayer
and the Church), 1879, 1880; "Arrows of the Chace," 2 vols., 1880;
"Elements of English Prosody," 1880; "The Bible of Amiens,"
1884 (first published in parts); "Love's Meinie" (Lectures delivered at Oxford, 1873-81), 1881; "Catalogue of Drawings and
Sketches by Turner in the National Gallery," 1881; "Catalogue
of Silicious Minerals at St. David's School, Reigate," 1883; "The
Art of England," 1884 (originally published as separate lectures);
"The Storm Cloud of the Nineteenth Century," 1884; "Catalogue
of Specimens of Silica in the British Museum," 1884; "Catalogue of Minerals given to Kirkcudbright Museum," 1884; "The
Pleasures of England" (Lectures delivered), 1844-5; "On the Old
Road," contributions to Periodical Literature, 2 vols., 1885;
"Præterita," 3 vols., 1885-9; "Dilecta," 1886-87; "Hortus
Inclusus," 1887; "Ruskiniana," 1890-92; "Poems" (Complete
edition), 1891; "Poetry of Architecture," 1892 (from the "Archi-
tectural Magazine").

"Stray Letters to a London Bibliophile," 1892; "Letters upon
Subjects of General Interest to various Correspondents," 1892;
"Letters to William Ward," 1893; "Letters addressed to a College
Friend," 1894; Separate Collections of Letters, edited by T. J.
Wise, were published 1894, 1895, 1896, and 1897; "Letters to
Charles Eliot Norton," edited by C. E. Norton, 1897; "Lectures
on Landscape," 1897; "Letters to Mary and Helen Gladstone,"
1903.

Works, in eleven volumes, 1871-83; Library Edition, edited by
E. T. Cook and A. Wedderburn, 1903, etc.

For Life, see W. G. Collingwood: "John Ruskin, a Biographical
Outline," 1889; "Life and Work of John Ruskin," 1893; "Life of
John Ruskin," 1900; Frederic Harrison: "Englishmen of Letters,"
1902.

CONTENTS

THE CROWN OF WILD OLIVE

PREFACE

Twenty years ago, there was no lovelier piece of low-land scenery in South England, nor any more pathetic, in the world, by its expression of sweet human character and life, than that immediately bordering on the sources of the Wandle, and including the lower moors of Addington, and the villages of Beddington and Carshalton, with all their pools and streams. No clearer or diviner waters ever sang with constant lips of the hand which " giveth rain from heaven; " no pastures ever lightened in spring time with more passionate blossoming; no sweeter homes ever hallowed the heart of the passer-by with their pride of peaceful gladness——fain-hidden—yet full-confessed. The place remains, or, until a few months ago, remained, nearly unchanged in its larger features; but, with deliberate mind I say, that I have never seen anything so ghastly in its inner tragic meaning,—not in Pisan Maremma,—not by Campagna tomb,—not by the sand-isles of the Torcellan shore,—as the slow stealing of aspects of reckless, indolent, animal neglect, over the delicate sweetness of that English scene: nor is any blasphemy or impiety—any frantic saying or godless thought—more appalling to me, using the best power of judgment I have to discern its sense and scope, than the insolent defiling of those springs by the human herds that drink of them. Just where the welling of stainless water, trembling and pure, like a body of light, enters the pool of Carshalton, cutting itself a radiant channel down to the gravel, through warp of feathery weeds, all waving, which it traverses with its deep threads of clearness, like the chalcedony in moss-agate, starred here and there with the white grenouillette; just in the very rush and murmur of the first spreading currents, the human wretches of the place cast their street and house foulness; heaps of dust and slime, and broken shreds of old metal, and rags of putrid clothes; they having neither energy to cart it away, nor decency enough to dig it into the ground, thus shed into the stream, to diffuse what venom of it will float and melt, far away, in all places where God meant those waters to bring joy and health. And, in a little pool, behind some houses farther in the village, where another spring rises, the shattered stones of the well, and of the little fretted channel which was long ago built and traced for it by gentler hands, lie scattered, each from each, under a ragged bank of mortar, and scoria; and bricklayers' refuse, on one side, which the clean water nevertheless chastises to purity; but it cannot conquer the dead earth beyond; and there, circled and coiled under festering scum, the stagnant edge of the pool effaces itself into a slope of black slime, the accumulation of indolent years. Half-a-dozen men, with one day's work, could cleanse those pools, and trim the flowers about their banks, and make every breath of summer air above them rich with cool balm; and every glittering wave medicinal, as if it ran, troubled of angels, from the porch of Bethesda. But that day's work is never given, nor will be; nor will any joy be possible to heart of man, for evermore, about those wells of English waters.

When I last left them, I walked up slowly through the back streets of Croydon, from the old church to the hospital; and, just on the left, before coming up to the crossing of the High Street, there was a new public-house built. And the front of it was built in so wise manner, that a recess of two feet was left below its front windows, between them and the street-pavement—a recess too narrow for any possible use, (for even if it had been occupied by a seat, as in old time it might have

been, everybody walking along the street would have
fallen over the legs of the reposing wayfarers). But, by
way of making this two feet depth of freehold land more
expressive of the dignity of an establishment for the
sale of spirituous liquors, it was fenced from the pave-
ment by an imposing iron railing, having four or five
spear-heads to the yard of it, and six feet high; containing as much iron and iron-work, indeed, as could well
be put into the space; and by this stately arrangement,
the little piece of dead ground within, between wall and
street, became a protective receptacle of refuse; cigar
ends, and oyster shells, and the like, such as an open-
handed English street-populace habitually scatters from
its presence, and was thus left, unsweepable by any
ordinary methods. Now the iron bars which, uselessly,
(or in great degree worse than uselessly) enclosed this
bit of ground, and made it pestilent, represented a
quantity of work which would have cleansed the
Carshalton pools three times over;—of work, partly
cramped and deadly, in the mine; partly fierce [1] and
exhaustive, at the furnace; partly foolish and seden-
tary, of ill-taught students making bad designs: work
from the beginning to the last fruits of it, and in all
the branches of it, venomous, deathful, and miserable.
Now, how did it come to pass that this work was done
instead of the other; that the strength and life of the

[1] " A fearful occurrence took place a few days since, near
Wolverhampton. Thomas Snape, aged nineteen, was on duty
as the ' keeper ' of a blast furnace at Deepfield, assisted by John
Gardner, aged eighteen, and Joseph Swift, aged thirty-seven.
The furnace contained four tons of molten iron, and an equal
amount of cinders, and ought to have been run out at 7.30 P.M.
But Snape and his mates, engaged in talking and drinking,
neglected their duty, and, in the meantime, the iron rose in the
furnace until it reached a pipe wherein water was contained.
Just as the men had stripped, and were proceeding to tap the
furnace, the water in the pipe, converted into steam, burst down
its front and let loose on them the molten metal, which instan-
taneously consumed Gardner; Snape, terribly burnt, and mad
with pain, leaped into the canal and then ran home and fell dead
on the threshold; Swift survived to reach the hospital, where he
died too."

English operative were spent in defiling ground, instead of redeeming it; and in producing an entirely (in that place) valueless piece of metal, which can neither be eaten nor breathed, instead of medicinal fresh air, and pure water?

There is but one reason for it, and at present a conclusive one,—that the capitalist can charge per-centage on the work in the one case, and cannot in the other. If, having certain funds for supporting labour at my disposal, I pay men merely to keep my ground in order, my money is, in that function, spent once for all; but if I pay them to dig iron out of my ground, and work it, and sell it, I can charge rent for the ground, and per-centage both on the manufacture and the sale, and make my capital profitable in these three bye-ways. The greater part of the profitable investment of capital, in the present day, is in operations of this kind, in which the public is persuaded to buy something of no use to it, on production, or sale, of which, the capitalist may charge per-centage; the said public remaining all the while under the persuasion that the per-centages thus obtained are real national gains, whereas, they are merely filchings out of partially light pockets, to swell heavy ones.

Thus, the Croydon publican buys the iron railing, to make himself more conspicuous to drunkards. The public-housekeeper on the other side of the way presently buys another railing, to out-rail him with. Both are, as to their *relative* attractiveness to customers of taste, just where they were before; but they have lost the price of the railings; which they must either themselves finally lose, or make their aforesaid customers of taste pay, by raising the price of their beer, or adulterating it. Either the publicans, or their customers, are thus poorer by precisely what the capitalist has gained; and the value of the work itself, meantime, has been lost to the nation; the iron bars in that form and place being wholly useless. It is this mode of taxation of the poor by the rich which is referred to in the text (page 32), in comparing the modern acquistive power of capital with that of the lance and sword; the only difference being that the levy of black mail in old times was by force, and is now by cozening. The old rider and reiver frankly quartered himself on the publican for the night; —the modern one merely makes his lance into an iron spike, and persuades his host to buy it. One comes as an open robber, the other as a cheating pedlar; but the result, to the injured person's pocket, is absolutely the same. Of course many useful industries mingle with, and disguise the useless ones; and in the habits of energy aroused by the struggle, there is a certain direct good. It is far better to spend four thousand pounds in making a good gun, and then to blow it to pieces, than to pass life in idleness. Only do not let it be called " political economy." There is also a confused notion in the minds of many persons, that the gathering of the property of the poor into the hands of the rich does no ultimate harm; since, in whosesoever hands it may be, it must be spent at last, and thus, they think, return to the poor again. This fallacy has been again and again exposed; but grant the plea true, and the same apology may, of course, be made for black mail, or any other form of robbery. It might be (though practically it never is) as advantageous for the nation that the robber should have the spending of the money he extorts, as that the person robbed should have spent it. But this is no excuse for the theft. If I were to put a turnpike on the road where it passes my own gate, and endeavour to exact a shilling from every passenger, the public would soon do away with my gate, without listening to any plea on my part that " it was as advantageous to them, in the end, that I should spend their shillings, as that they themselves should." But if, instead of out-facing them with a turnpike, I can only persuade them to come in and buy stones, or old iron, or any other use-less thing, out of my ground, I may rob them to the same extent, and be, moreover, thanked as a public benefactor, and promoter of commercial prosperity. And this main question for the poor of England—for the poor of all countries—is wholly omitted in every common treatise on the subject of wealth. Even by the labourers themselves, the operation of capital is regarded only in its effect on their immediate interests; never in the far more terrific power of its appointment of the kind and the object of labour. It matters little, ultimately, how much a labourer is paid for making anything; but it matters fearfully what the thing is, which he is compelled to make. If his labour is so ordered as to produce food, and fresh air, and fresh water, no matter that his wages are low;—the food and fresh air and water will be at last there; and he will at last get them. But if he is paid to destroy food and fresh air, or to produce iron bars instead of them,—the food and air will finally *not* be there, and he will *not* get them, to his great and final inconvenience. So that, conclusively, in political as in household economy, the great question is, not so much what money you have in your pocket, as what you will buy with it, and do with it.

I have been long accustomed, as all men engaged in work of investigation must be, to hear my statements laughed at for years, before they are examined or believed; and I am generally content to wait the public's time. But it has not been without displeased surprise that I have found myself totally unable, as yet, by any repetition, or illustration, to force this plain thought into my readers' heads,—that the wealth of nations, as of men, consists in substance, not in ciphers; and that the real good of all work, and of all commerce, depends on the final worth of the thing you make, or get by it. This is a practical enough statement, one would think: but the English public has been so possessed by its modern school of economists with the notion that Business is always good, whether it be busy

in mischief or in benefit; and that buying and selling
are always salutary, whatever the intrinsic worth of
what you buy or sell,—that it seems impossible to gain
so much as a patient hearing for any inquiry respecting
the substantial result of our eager modern labours. I
have never felt more checked by the sense of this impossibility than in arranging the heads of the following
three lectures, which, though delivered at considerable
intervals of time, and in different places, were not
prepared without reference to each other. Their
connection would, however, have been made far
more distinct, if I had not been prevented, by what I
feel to be another great difficulty in addressing English audiences, from enforcing, with any decision, the
common, and to me the most important, part of their
subjects. I chiefly desired (as I have just said) to question my hearers—operatives, merchants, and soldiers,
as to the ultimate meaning of the *business* they had in
hand; and to know from them what they expected or
intended their manufacture to come to, their selling to
come to, and their killing to come to. That appeared
the first point needing determination before I could
speak to them with any real utility or effect. " You
craftsmen — salesmen — swordsmen, — do but tell me
clearly what you want; then, if I can say anything to
help you, I will; and if not, I will account to you as I
best may for my inability." But in order to put this
question into any terms, one had first of all to face the
difficulty just spoken of—to me for the present insuper
able,—the difficulty of knowing whether to address
one's audience as believing, or not believing, in any
other world than this. For if you address any average
modern English company as believing in an Eternal
life, and endeavour to draw any conclusions, from this
assumed belief, as to their present business, they will
forthwith tell you that " what you say is very beautiful,
but it is not practical." If, on the contrary, you frankly
address them as unbelievers in Eternal life, and try to

draw any consequences from that unbelief,—they immediately hold you for an accursed person, and shake off the dust from their feet at you. And the more I thought over what I had got to say, the less I found I could say it, without some reference to this intangible or intractable part of the subject. It made all the difference, in asserting any principle of war, whether one assumed that a discharge of artillery would merely knead down a certain quantity of red clay into a level line, as in a brick-field; or whether, out of every separately Christian-named portion of the ruinous heap, there went out, into the smoke and dead-fallen air of battle, some astonished condition of soul, unwillingly released. It made all the difference, in speaking of the possible range of commerce, whether one assumed that all bargains related only to visible property—or whether property, for the present invisible, but nevertheless real, was elsewhere purchasable on other terms. It made all the difference, in addressing a body of men subject to considerable hardship, and having to find some way out of it—whether one could confidently say to them, " My friends,—you have only to die, and all will be right; " or whether one had any secret misgiving that such advice was more blessed to him that gave, than to him that took it. And therefore the deliberate reader will find, throughout these lectures, a hesitation in driving points home, and a pausing short of conclusions which he will feel I would fain have come to; hesitation which arises wholly from this uncertainty of my hearers' temper. For I do not now speak, nor have I ever spoken, since the time of first forward youth, in any proselyting temper, as desiring to persuade any one of what, in such matters, I thought myself; but, whomsoever I venture to address, I take for the time his creed as I find it; and endeavour to push it into such vital fruit as it seems capable of. Thus, it is a creed with a great part of the existing English people, that they are in possession of a book which tells them, straight from the lips of God, all they ought to do, and need to know. I have read that book, with as much care as most of them, for some forty years; and am thankful that, on those who trust it, I can press its pleadings. My endeavour has been uniformly to make them trust it more deeply than they do; trust it, not in their own favourite verses only, but in the sum of all; trust it, not as a fetish or talisman, which they are to be saved by daily repetitions of; but as a Captain's order, to be heard and obeyed at their peril. I was always encouraged by supposing my hearers to hold such belief. To these, if to any, I once had hope of addressing, with acceptance, words which insisted on the guilt of pride, and the futility of avarice; from these, if from any, I once expected ratification of a political economy, which asserted that the life was more than the meat, and the body than raiment; and these, it once seemed to me, I might ask, without accusation of fanaticism, not merely in doctrine of the lips, but in the bestowal of their heart's treasure, to separate themselves from the crowd of whom it is written, " After all these things do the Gentiles seek."

It cannot, however, be assumed, with any semblance of reason, that a general audience is now wholly, or even in majority, composed of these religious persons. A large portion must always consist of men who admit no such creed; or who, at least, are inaccessible to appeals founded on it. And as, with the so-called Christian, I desired to plead for honest declaration and fulfilment of his belief in life,—with the so-called Infidel, I desired to plead for an honest declaration and fulfilment of his belief in death. The dilemma is inevitable. Men must either hereafter live, or hereafter die; fate may be bravely met, and conduct wisely ordered, on either expectation; but never in hesitation between ungrasped hope, and unconfronted fear. We usually believe in immortality, so far as to avoid preparation for death; and in mortality, so far as to avoid preparation for anything after death. Whereas, a wise man will at least hold himself prepared for one or other of two events, of which one or other is inevitable; and will have all things in order, for his sleep, or in readiness, for his awakening.

Nor have we any right to call it an ignoble judgment, if he determine to put them in order, as for sleep. A brave belief in life is indeed an enviable state of mind, but, as far as I can discern, an unusual one. I know few Christians so convinced of the splendour of the rooms in their Father's house, as to be happier when their friends are called to those mansions, than they would have been if the Queen had sent for them to live at court: nor has the Church's most ardent " desire to depart, and be with Christ," ever cured it of the singular habit of putting on mourning for every person summoned to such departure. On the contrary, a brave belief in death has been assuredly held by many not ignoble persons, and it is a sign of the last depravity in the Church itself, when it assumes that such a belief is inconsistent with either purity of character, or energy of hand. The shortness of life is not, to any rational person, a conclusive reason for wasting the space of it which may be granted him; nor does the anticipation of death to-morrow suggest, to any one but a drunkard, the expediency of drunkenness to-day. To teach that there is no device in the grave, may indeed make the deviceless person more contented in his dulness; but it will make the deviser only more earnest in devising: nor is human conduct likely, in every case, to be purer, under the conviction that all its evil may in a moment be pardoned, and all its wrong-doing in a moment redeemed; and that the sigh of repentance, which purges the guilt of the past, will waft the soul into a felicity which forgets its pain, —than it may be under the sterner, and to many not unwise minds, more probable, apprehension, that " what a man soweth that shall he also reap "—or others reap,—when he, the living seed of pestilence, walketh no more in darkness, but lies down therein.

But to men whose feebleness of sight, or bitterness of soul, or the offence given by the conduct of those who claim higher hope, may have rendered this painful creed the only possible one, there is an appeal to be made, more secure in its ground than any which can be addressed to happier persons. I would fain, if I might offencelessly, have spoken to them as if none others heard; and have said thus: Hear me, you dying men, who will soon be deaf for ever. For these others, at your right hand and your left, who look forward to a state of infinite existence, in which all their errors will be overruled, and all their faults forgiven; for these, who, stained and blackened in the battle smoke of mortality, have but to dip themselves for an instant in the font of death, and to rise renewed of plumage, as a dove that is covered with silver, and her feathers like gold; for these, indeed, it may be permissible to waste their numbered moments, through faith in a future of innumerable hours; to these, in their weakness, it may be conceded that they should tamper with sin which can only bring forth fruit of righteousness, and profit by the iniquity which, one day, will be remembered no more. In them, it may be no sign of hardness of heart to neglect the poor, over whom they know their Master is watching; and to leave those to perish temporarily, who cannot perish eternally. But, for you, there is no such hope, and therefore no such excuse. This fate, which you ordain for the wretched, you believe to be all their inheritance; you may crush them, before the moth, and they will never rise to rebuke you;—their breath, which fails for lack of food, once expiring, will never be recalled to whisper against you a word of accusing;—they and you, as you think, shall lie down together in the dust, and the worms cover you;—and for them there shall be no consolation, and on you no vengeance,—only the question murmured

above your grave: " Who shall repay him what he hath
done?" Is it therefore easier for you in your heart
to inflict the sorrow for which there is no remedy?
Will you take, wantonly, this little all of his life from
your poor brother, and make his brief hours long to him
with pain? Will you be readier to the injustice which
can never be redressed; and niggardly of mercy which
you *can* bestow but once, and which, refusing, you
refuse for ever? I think better of you, even of the
most selfish, than that you would do this, well understood. And for yourselves, it seems to me, the question becomes not less grave, in these curt limits. If
your life were but a fever fit,—the madness of a night,
whose follies were all to be forgotten in the dawn, it
might matter little how you fretted away the sickly
hours,—what toys you snatched at, or let fall,—what
visions you followed wistfully with the deceived eyes
of sleepless phrenzy. Is the earth only an hospital?
Play, if you care to play, on the floor of the hospital
dens. Knit its straw into what crowns please you;
gather the dust of it for treasure, and die rich in that,
clutching at the black motes in the air with your dying
hands;—and yet, it may be well with you. But if
this life be no dream, and the world no hospital; if all
the peace and power and joy you can ever win, must
be won now; and all fruit of victory gathered here,
or never;—will you still, throughout the puny totality
of your life, weary yourselves in the fire for vanity?
If there is no rest which remaineth for you, is there
none you might presently take? was this grass of the
earth made green for your shroud only, not for your
bed? and can you never lie down *upon* it, but only
under it? The heathen, to whose creed you have
returned, thought not so. They knew that life brought
its contest, but they expected from it also the crown
of all contest: No proud one! no jewelled circlet
flaming through Heaven above the height of the un-
merited throne; only some few leaves of wild olive,

cool to the tired brow, through a few years of peace. It should have been of gold, they thought; but Jupiter was poor; this was the best the god could give them. Seeking a greater than this, they had known it a mockery. Not in war, not in wealth, not in tyranny, was there any happiness to be found for them—only in kindly peace, fruitful and free. The wreath was to be of *wild* olive, mark you:—the tree that grows carelessly, tufting the rocks with no vivid bloom, no verdure of branch; only with soft snow of blossom, and scarcely fulfilled fruit, mixed with grey leaf and thorn-set stem; no fastening of diadem for you but with such sharp embroidery! But this, such as it is, you may win while yet you live; type of grey honour and sweet rest.[1] Free-heartedness, and graciousness, and undisturbed trust, and requited love, and the sight of the peace of others, and the ministry to their pain;—these, and the blue sky above you, and the sweet waters and flowers of the earth beneath; and mysteries and presences, innumerable, of living things,—these may yet be here your riches; untormenting and divine: serviceable for the life that now is; nor, it may be, without promise of that which is to come.

[1] μελιτόεσσα, ἀέθλων γ᾽ ἕνεκεν.

LECTURE I

WORK

LECTURE I

(Delivered before the Working Men's Institute, at Camberwell.)

MY FRIENDS,—I have not come among you to-night to endeavour to give you an entertaining lecture; but to tell you a few plain facts, and ask you some plain, but necessary, questions. I have seen and known too much of the struggle for life among our labouring population, to feel at ease, even under any circumstances, in inviting them to dwell on the trivialities of my own studies; but, much more, as I meet to-night, for the first time, the members of a working Institute established in the district in which I have passed the greater part of my life, I am desirous that we should at once understand each other, on graver matters. I would fain tell you, with what feelings, and with what hope, I regard this Institution, as one of many such, now happily established throughout England, as well as in other countries;— Institutions which are preparing the way for a great change in all the circumstances of industrial life; but of which the success must wholly depend upon our clearly understanding the circumstances and necessary *limits* of this change. No teacher can truly promote the cause of education, until he knows the conditions of the life for which that education is to prepare his pupil. And the fact that he is called upon to address you, nominally, as a " Working Class," must compel him, if he is in any wise earnest or thoughtful, to enquire in

19

the outset, on what you yourselves suppose this class distinction has been founded in the past, and must be founded in the future. The manner of the amusement, and the matter of the teaching, which any of us can offer you, must depend wholly on our first understanding from you, whether you think the distinction heretofore drawn between working men and others, is truly or falsely founded. Do you accept it as it stands? do you wish it to be modified? or do you think the object of education is to efface it, and make us forget it for ever?

Let me make myself more distinctly understood. We call this—you and I—a " Working Men's " Institute, and our college in London, a " Working Men's " College. Now, how do you consider that these several institutes differ, or ought to differ, from " idle men's " institutes and " idle men's " colleges? Or by what other word than " idle " shall I distinguish those whom the happiest and wisest of working men do not object to call the " Upper Classes "? Are there really upper classes,— are there lower? How much should they always be elevated, how much always depressed? And, gentlemen and ladies—I pray those of you who are here to forgive me the offence there may be in what I am going to say. It is not *I* who wish to say it. Bitter voices say it; voices of battle and of famine through all the world, which must be heard some day, whoever keeps silence. Neither is it to *you* specially that I say it. I am sure that most now present know their duties of kindness, and fulfil them, better perhaps than I do mine. But I speak to you as representing your whole class, which errs, I know, chiefly by thoughtlessness, but not therefore the less terribly. Wilful error is limited by the will, but what limit is there to that of which we are unconscious?

Bear with me, therefore, while I turn to these workmen, and ask them, also as representing a great multitude, what they think the " upper classes " are, and

ought to be, in relation to them. Answer, you workmen who are here, as you would among yourselves,
frankly; and tell me how you would have me call those
classes. Am I to call them—would *you* think me right
in calling them—the idle classes? I think you would
feel somewhat uneasy, and as if I were not treating my
subject honestly, or speaking from my heart, if I went
on under the supposition that all rich people were idle.
You would be both unjust and unwise if you allowed me
to say that;—not less unjust than the rich people who
say that all the poor are idle, and will never work if they
can help it, or more than they can help.

For indeed the fact is, that there are idle poor and idle
rich; and there are busy poor and busy rich. Many a
beggar is as lazy as if he had ten thousand a year; and
many a man of large fortune is busier than his errand-
boy, and never would think of stopping in the street to
play marbles. So that, in a large view, the distinction
between workers and idlers, as between knaves and
honest men, runs through the very heart and innermost
economies of men of all ranks and in all positions.
There is a working class—strong and happy,—among
both rich and poor; there is an idle class—weak, wicked,
and miserable,—among both rich and poor. And the
worst of the misunderstandings arising between the two
orders come of the unlucky fact that the wise of one
class habitually contemplate the foolish of the other. If
the busy rich people watched and rebuked the idle rich
people, all would be right: and if the busy poor people
watched and rebuked the idle poor people, all would be
right. But each class has a tendency to look for the
faults of the other. A hard-working man of property
is particularly offended by an idle beggar; and an
orderly, but poor, workman is naturally intolerant of
the licentious luxury of the rich. And what is severe
judgment in the minds of the just men of either class,
becomes fierce enmity in the unjust—but among the
unjust *only*. None but the dissolute among the poor

look upon the rich as their natural enemies, or desire to
pillage their houses and divide their property.   None
but the dissolute among the rich speak in opprobrious
terms of the vices and follies of the poor.

There is, then, no class distinction between idle and
industrious people; and I am going to-night to speak
only of the industrious.   The idle people we will put
out of our thoughts at once—they are mere nuisances
—what ought to be done with *them*, we'll talk of at
another time.   But there are class distinctions among
the industrious themselves;—tremendous distinctions,
which rise and fall to every degree in the infinite
thermometer of human pain and of human power,—
distinctions of high and low, of lost and won, to the
whole reach of man's soul and body.

These separations we will study, and the laws of them,
among energetic men only, who, whether they work
or whether they play, put their strength into the work,
and their strength into the game; being in the full
sense of the word "industrious," one way or another,
—with purpose, or without.   And these distinctions
are mainly four:

I. Between those who work, and those who play.

II. Between those who produce the means of life, and
those who consume them.

III. Between those who work with the head, and
those who work with the hand.

IV. Between those who work wisely, and who work
foolishly.

For easier memory, let us say we are going to oppose,
in our examination,—

    I. Work to play;

    II. Production to consumption;

    III. Head to hand; and,

    IV. Sense to nonsense.

I. First, then, of the distinction between the classes

who work and the classes who play. Of course we must agree upon a definition of these terms,—work and play, —before going farther. Now, roughly, not with vain subtlety of definition, but for plain use of the words, " play " is an exertion of body or mind, made to please ourselves, and with no determined end; and work is a thing done because it ought to be done, and with a determined end. You play, as you call it, at cricket, for instance. That is as hard work as anything else; but it amuses you, and it has no result but the amusement. If it were done as an ordered form of exercise, for health's sake, it would become work directly. So, in like manner, whatever we do to please ourselves, and only for the sake of the pleasure, not for an ultimate object, is " play," the " pleasing thing," not the useful thing. Play may be useful, in a secondary sense; (nothing is indeed more useful or necessary); but the use of it depends on its being spontaneous.

Let us, then, enquire together what sort of games the playing class in England spend their lives in playing at.

The first of all English games is making money. That is an all-absorbing game; and we knock each other down oftener in playing at that, than at football, or any other roughest sport: and it is absolutely without purpose; no one who engages heartily in that game ever knows why. Ask a great money-maker what he wants to do with his money,—he never knows. He doesn't make it to do anything with it. He gets it only that he *may* get it. " What will you make of what you have got? " you ask. " Well, I'll get more," he says. Just as, at cricket, you get more runs. There's no use in the runs, but to get more of them than other people is the game. And there's no use in the money, but to have more of it than other people is the game. So all that great foul city of London there, —rattling, growling, smoking, stinking,—a ghastly heap of fermenting brickwork, pouring out poison at

every pore,—you fancy it is a city of work? Not a
street of it! It is a great city of play; very nasty play,
and very hard play, but still play. It is only Lord's
cricket ground without the turf:—a huge billiard table
without the cloth, and with pockets as deep as the
bottomless pit; but mainly a billiard table, after all.

Well, the first great English game is this playing at
counters. It differs from the rest in that it appears
always to be producing money, while every other game
is expensive. But it does not always produce money.
There's a great difference between " winning " money
and " making " it: a great difference between getting
it out of another man's pocket into ours, or filling both.
Collecting money is by no means the same thing as
making it; the tax-gatherer's house is not the Mint;
and much of the apparent gain, (so called), in commerce,
is only a form of taxation on carriage or exchange.

Our next great English game, however, hunting and
shooting, is costly altogether; and how much we are
fined for it annually in land, horses, gamekeepers, and
game laws, and all else that accompanies that beautiful
and special English game, I will not endeavour to
count now; but note only that, except for exercise,
this is not merely a useless game, but a deadly one, to
all connected with it. For through horse-racing, you
get every form of what the higher classes everywhere
call " Play," in distinction from all other plays; that
is,—gambling; by no means a beneficial or recreative
game: and, through game-preserving, you get also
some curious laying out of ground; that beautiful
arrangement of dwelling-house for man and beast, by
which we have grouse and blackcock—so many brace
to the acre, and men and women—so many brace to
the garret. I often wonder what the angelic builders
and surveyors—the angelic builders who build the
" many mansions " up above there; and the angelic
surveyors, who measured that four-square city with
their measuring reeds—I wonder what they think, or

are supposed to think, of the laying out of ground by this nation, which has set itself, as it seems, literally to accomplish, word for word, or rather fact for word, in the persons of those poor whom its Master left to represent him, what that Master said of himself—that foxes and birds had homes, but He none.

Then, next to the gentlemen's game of hunting, we must put the ladies' game of dressing. It is not the cheapest of games. I saw a brooch at a jeweller's in Bond Street a fortnight ago, not an inch wide, and without any singular jewel in it, yet worth £3000. And I wish I could tell you what this " play " costs, altogether, in England, France, and Russia annually. But it is a pretty game, and on certain terms, I like it; nay, I don't see it played quite as much as I would fain have it. You ladies like to lead the fashion:—by all means lead it—lead it thoroughly, lead it far enough. Dress yourselves nicely, and dress everybody else nicely. Lead the *fashions for the poor* first; make *them* look well, and you yourselves will look, in ways of which you have now no conception, all the better. The fashions you have set for some time among your peasantry are not pretty ones; their doublets are too irregularly slashed, and the wind blows too frankly through them.

Then there are other games, wild enough, as I could show you if I had time.

There's playing at literature, and playing at art—very different, both, from working at literature, or working at art, but I've no time to speak of these. I pass to the greatest of all—the play of plays, the great gentleman's game, which ladies like them best to play at,—the game of War. It is entrancingly pleasant to the imagination; the facts of it, not always so pleasant. We dress for it, however, more finely than for any other sport; and go out to it, not merely in scarlet, as to hunt, but in scarlet and gold, and all manner of fine colours: of course we could fight better in grey, and without feathers; but all nations have agreed that it is good to be well dressed at this play. Then the bats and balls are very costly; our English and French bats, with the balls and wickets, even those which we don't make any use of, costing, I suppose, now about fifteen millions of money annually to each nation; all which you know is paid for by hard labourer's work in the furrow and furnace. A costly game!—not to speak of its consequences; I will say at present nothing of these. The mere immediate cost of all these plays is what I want you to consider; they all cost deadly work somewhere, as many of us know too well. The jewel-cutter, whose sight fails over the diamonds; the weaver, whose arm fails over the web; the iron-forger, whose breath fails before the furnace—*they* know what work is—they, who have all the work, and none of the play, except a kind they have named for themselves down in the black north country, where " play " means being laid up by sickness. It is a pretty example for philologists, of varying dialect, this change in the sense of the word " play," as used in the black country of Birmingham, and the red and black country of Baden Baden. Yes, gentlemen, and gentlewomen, of England, who think " one moment unamused a misery, not made for feeble man," this is what you have brought the word " play " to mean, in the heart of merry England! You may have your fluting and piping; but there are sad children sitting in the market-place, who indeed cannot say to you, " We have piped unto you, and ye have not danced: " but eternally shall say to you, " We have mourned unto you, and ye have not lamented."

This, then, is the first distinction between the " upper and lower " classes. And this is one which is by no means necessary; which indeed must, in process of good time, be by all honest men's consent abolished. Men will be taught that an existence of play, sustained by the blood of other creatures, is a good existence for gnats and sucking fish; but not for men: that neither days, nor lives, can be made holy by doing nothing in

them: that the best prayer at the beginning of a day
is that we may not lose its moments; and the best grace
before meat, the consciousness that we have justly
earned our dinner. And when we have this much of
plain Christianity preached to us again, and enough
respect what we regard as inspiration, as not to think
that " Son, go work to-day in my vineyard," means
" Fool, go play to-day in my vineyard," we shall all be
workers, in one way or another; and this much at least
of the distinction between " upper " and " lower "
forgotten.

II. I pass then to our second distinction; between
the rich and poor, between Dives and Lazarus,—
distinction which exists more sternly, I suppose, in this
day, than ever in the world, Pagan or Christian, till
now. I will put it sharply before you, to begin with,
merely by reading two paragraphs which I cut from
two papers that lay on my breakfast table on the same
morning, the 25th of November, 1864. The piece about
the rich Russian at Paris is common-place enough, and
stupid besides; (for fifteen francs—12s. 6d.,—is nothing
for a rich man to give for a couple of peaches, out of
season). Still, the two paragraphs printed on the same
day are worth putting side by side.

" Such a man is now here. He is a Russian, and,
with your permission, we will call him Count Teufel-
skine. In dress he is sublime; art is considered in that
toilet, the harmony of colour respected, the *chiar'
oscuro* evident in well-selected contrast. In manners he
is dignified—nay, perhaps apathetic; nothing disturbs
the placid serenity of that calm exterior. One day our
friend breakfasted *chez* Bignon. When the bill came
he read, ' Two peaches, 15f.' He paid. ' Peaches
scarce, I presume?' was his sole remark. ' No, sir,'
replied the waiter, ' but Teufelskines are.' "—*Telegraph*,
November 25, 1864.

" Yesterday morning, at eight o'clock, a woman,
passing a dung heap in the stone yard near the recently-

erected alms-houses in Shadwell Gap, High Street, Shadwell, called the attention of a Thames police-constable to a man in a sitting position on the dung heap, and said she was afraid he was dead. Her fears proved to be true. The wretched creature appeared to have been dead several hours. He had perished of cold and wet, and the rain had been beating down on him all night. The deceased was a bone-picker. He was in the lowest stage of poverty, poorly clad, and half-starved. The police had frequently driven him away from the stone yard, between sunset and sunrise, and told him to go home. He selected a most desolate spot for his wretched death. A penny and some bones were found in his pockets. The deceased was between fifty and sixty years of age. Inspector Roberts, of the K division, has given directions for inquiries to be made at the lodging-houses respecting the deceased, to ascertain his identity if possible."—*Morning Post*, November 25, 1864.

You have the separation thus in brief compass; and I want you to take notice of the " a penny and some bones were found in his pockets," and to compare it with this third statement, from the *Telegraph* of January 16th of this year:—

" Again, the dietary scale for adult and juvenile paupers was drawn up by the most conspicuous political economists in England. It is low in quantity, but it is sufficient to support nature; yet within ten years of the passing of the Poor Law Act, we heard of the paupers in the Andover Union gnawing the scraps of putrid flesh and sucking the marrow from the bones of horses which they were employed to crush."

You see my reason for thinking that our Lazarus of Christianity has some advantage over the Jewish one. Jewish Lazarus expected, or at least prayed, to be fed with crumbs from the rich man's table; but *our* Lazarus is fed with crumbs from the dog's table.

Now this distinction between rich and poor rests on

two bases. Within its proper limits, on a basis which is lawful and everlastingly necessary; beyond them, on a basis unlawful, and everlastingly corrupting the framework of society. The lawful basis of wealth is, that a man who works should be paid the fair value of his work; and that if he does not choose to spend it to-day, he should have free leave to keep it, and spend it to-morrow. Thus, an industrious man working daily, and laying by daily, attains at last the possession of an accumulated sum of wealth, to which he has absolute right. The idle person who will not work, and the wasteful person who lays nothing by, at the end of the same time will be doubly poor—poor in possession, and dissolute in moral habit; and he will then naturally covet the money which the other has saved. And if he is then allowed to attack the other, and rob him of his well-earned wealth, there is no more any motive for saving, or any reward for good conduct; and all society is thereupon dissolved, or exists only in systems of rapine. Therefore the first necessity of social life is the clearness of national conscience in enforcing the law— that he should keep who has JUSTLY EARNED.

That law, I say, is the proper basis of distinction between rich and poor. But there is also a false basis of distinction; namely, the power held over those who earn wealth by those who levy or exact it. There will be always a number of men who would fain set themselves to the accumulation of wealth as the sole object of their lives. Necessarily, that class of men is an uneducated class, inferior in intellect, and more or less cowardly. It is physically impossible for a well-educated, intellectual, or brave man to make money the chief object of his thoughts; as physically impossible as it is for him to make his dinner the principal object of them. All healthy people like their dinners, but their dinner is not the main object of their lives. So all healthily minded people like making money—ought to like it, and to enjoy the sensation of winning it: but the main object of their life is not money; it is something better than money. A good soldier, for instance, mainly wishes to do his fighting well. He is glad of his pay—very properly so, and justly grumbles when you keep him ten years without it—still, his main notion of life is to win battles, not to be paid for winning them. So of clergymen. They like pew-rents, and baptismal fees, of course; but yet, if they are brave and well educated, the pew-rent is not the sole object of their lives, and the baptismal fee is not the sole purpose of the baptism; the clergyman's object is essentially to baptise and preach, not to be paid for preaching. So of doctors. They like fees no doubt,—ought to like them; yet if they are brave and well educated, the entire object of their lives is not fees. They, on the whole, desire to cure the sick; and,—if they are good doctors, and the choice were fairly put to them,—would rather cure their patient, and lose their fee, than kill him, and get it. And so with all other brave and rightly trained men; their work is first, their fee second—very important always, but still *second*. But in every nation, as I said, there are a vast class who are ill-educated, cowardly, and more or less stupid. And with these people, just as certainly the fee is first, and the work second, as with brave people the work is first and the fee second. And this is no small distinction. It is the whole distinction in a man; distinction between life and death *in* him, between heaven and hell *for* him. You cannot serve two masters;—you *must* serve one or other. If your work is first with you, and your fee second, work is your master, and the lord of work, who is God. But if your fee is first with you, and your work second, fee is your master, and the lord of fee, who is the Devil; and not only the Devil, but the lowest of devils—the " least erected fiend that fell." So there you have it in brief terms; Work first—you are God's servants; Fee first— you are the Fiend's. And it makes a difference, now and ever, believe me, whether you serve Him who has

on His vesture and thigh written, " King of Kings,"
and whose service is perfect freedom; or him on whose
vesture and thigh the name is written, " Slave of
Slaves," and whose service is perfect slavery.

However, in every nation there are, and must always
be, a certain number of these Fiend's servants, who have
it principally for the object of their lives to make money.
They are always, as I said, more or less stupid, and
cannot conceive of anything else so nice as money.
Stupidity is always the basis of the Judas bargain.   We
do great injustice to Iscariot, in thinking him wicked
above all common wickedness.   He was only a common
money-lover, and, like all money-lovers, didn't understand Christ;—couldn't make out the worth of Him, or
meaning of Him.   He didn't want Him to be killed.
He was horror-struck when he found that Christ would
be killed; threw his money away instantly, and hanged
himself.   How many of our present money-seekers,
think you, would have the grace to hang themselves, whoever was killed?   But Judas was a common,
selfish, muddle-headed, pilfering fellow; his hand
always in the bag of the poor, not caring for them.
He didn't understand Christ;—yet believed in Him,
much more than most of us do; had seen Him do
miracles, thought He was quite strong enough to shift
for Himself, and he, Judas, might as well make his own
little bye-perquisites out of the affair.   Christ would
come out of it well enough, and he have his thirty pieces.
Now, that is the money-seeker's idea, all over the world.
He doesn't hate Christ, but can't understand Him—
doesn't care for Him—sees no good in that benevolent
business; makes his own little job out of it at all events,
come what will.   And thus, out of every mass of men,
you have a certain number of bagmen—your " fee-first "
men, whose main object is to make money.   And they
do make it—make it in all sorts of unfair ways, chiefly
by the weight and force of money itself, or what is
called the power of capital; that is to say, the power

which money, once obtained, has over the labour of the
poor, so that the capitalist can take all its produce to
himself, except the labourer's food.   That is the modern
Judas's way of " carrying the bag," and " bearing what
is put therein."

Nay, but (it is asked) how is that an unfair advantage?
Has not the man who has worked for the money a right
to use it as he best can?   No; in this respect, money
is now exactly what mountain promontories over public
roads were in old times.   The barons fought for them
fairly:—the strongest and cunningest got them; then
fortified them, and made every one who passed below
pay toll.   Well, capital now is exactly what crags were
then.   Men fight fairly (we will, at least, grant so much,
though it is more than we ought) for their money: but,
once having got it, the fortified millionaire can make
everybody who passes below pay toll to his million, and
build another tower of his money castle.   And I can
tell you, the poor vagrants by the roadside suffer now
quite as much from the bag-baron, as ever they did
from the crag-baron.   Bags and crags have just the
same result on rags.   I have not time, however, to-
night to show you in how many ways the power of
capital is unjust: but this one great principle I have to
assert—you will find it quite indisputably true—that
whenever money is the principal object of life with
either man or nation, it is both got ill, and spent ill; and
does harm both in the getting and spending; but when
it is not the principal object, it and all other things will
be well got, and well spent.   And here is the test, with
every man, of whether money is the principal object
with him, or not.   If in mid-life he could pause and say,
" Now I have enough to live upon, I'll live upon it; and
having well earned it, I will also well spend it, and go
out of the world poor, as I came into it," then money is
not principal with him; but if, having enough to live
upon in the manner befitting his character and rank, he
still wants to make more, and to *die* rich, then money is

the principal object with him, and it becomes a curse to himself, and generally to those who spend it after him. For you know it *must* be spent some day; the only question is whether the man who makes it shall spend it, or some one else. And generally it is better for the maker to spend it, for he will know best its value and use. This is the true law of life. And if a man does not choose thus to spend his money, he must either hoard it or lend it, and the worst thing he can generally do is to lend it; for borrowers are nearly always ill-spenders, and it is with lent money that all evil is mainly done, and all unjust war protracted.

For observe what the real fact is, respecting loans to foreign military governments, and how strange it is. If your little boy came to you to ask for money to spend in squibs and crackers, you would think twice before you gave it him; and you would have some idea that it was wasted, when you saw it fly off in fireworks, even though he did no mischief with it. But the Russian children, and Austrian children, come to you, borrowing money, not to spend in innocent squibs, but in cartridges and bayonets to attack you in India with, and to keep down all noble life in Italy with, and to murder Polish women and children with; and *that* you will give at once, because they pay you interest for it. Now, in order to pay you that interest, they must tax every working peasant in their dominions; and on that work you live. You therefore at once rob the Austrian peasant, assassinate or banish the Polish peasant, and you live on the produce of the theft, and the bribe for the assassination! That is the broad fact—that is the practical meaning of your foreign loans, and of most large interest of money; and then you quarrel with Bishop Colenso, forsooth, as if *he* denied the Bible, and you believed it! though, wretches as you are, every deliberate act of your lives is a new defiance of its primary orders; and as if, for most of the rich men of England at this moment, it were not indeed to be desired, as the best thing at least for *them,* that the Bible should *not* be true, since against them these words are written in it: " The rust of your gold and silver shall be a witness against you, and shall eat your flesh, as it were fire."

III. I pass now to our third condition of separation, between the men who work with the hand, and those who work with the head.

And here we have at last an inevitable distinction. There *must* be work done by the arms, or none of us could live. There *must* be work done by the brains, or the life we get would not be worth having. And the same men cannot do both. There is rough work to be done, and rough men must do it; there is gentle work to be done, and gentlemen must do it; and it is physically impossible that one class should do, or divide, the work of the other. And it is of no use to try to conceal this sorrowful fact by fine words, and to talk to the workmen about the honourableness of manual labour, and the dignity of humanity. That is a grand old proverb of Sancho Panza's, " Fine words butter no parsnips; " and I can tell you that, all over England just now, you workmen are buying a great deal too much butter at that dairy. Rough work, honourable or not, takes the life out of us; and the man who has been heaving clay out of a ditch all day, or driving an express train against the north wind all night, or holding a collier's helm in a gale on a lee shore, or whirling white-hot iron at a furnace mouth, that man is not the same at the end of his day, or night, as one who has been sitting in a quiet room, with everything comfortable about him, reading books, or classing butterflies, or painting pictures. If it is any comfort to you to be told that the rough work is the more honourable of the two, I should be sorry to take that much of consolation from you; and in some sense I need not. The rough work is at all events real, honest, and, generally, though not always, useful; while the fine work is, a great deal of it, foolish and false as well as fine, and therefore dishonourable: but when both kinds are equally well and worthily done, the head's is the noble work, and the hand's the ignoble; and of all hand work whatsoever, necessary for the maintenance of life, these old words, " In the sweat of thy face thou shalt eat bread," indicate that the inherent nature of it is one of calamity; and that the ground, cursed for our sake, casts also some shadow of degradation into our contest with its thorn and its thistle: so that all nations have held their days honourable, or " holy," and constituted them " holydays," or " holidays," by making them days of rest; and the promise, which, among all our distant hopes, seems to cast the chief brightness over death, is that blessing of the dead who die in the Lord, that " they rest from their labours, and their works do follow them."

And thus the perpetual question and contest must arise, who is to do this rough work? and how is the worker of it to be comforted, redeemed, and rewarded? and what kind of play should he have, and what rest, in this world, sometimes, as well as in the next? Well, my good working friends, these questions will take a little time to answer yet. They must be answered: all good men are occupied with them, and all honest thinkers. There's grand head work doing about them; but much must be discovered, and much attempted in vain, before anything decisive can be told you. Only note these few particulars, which are already sure.

As to the distribution of the hard work. None of us, or very few of us, do either hard or soft work because we think we ought; but because we have chanced to fall into the way of it, and cannot help ourselves. Now, nobody does anything well that they cannot help doing: work is only done well when it is done with a will; and no man has a thoroughly sound will unless he knows he is doing what he should, and is in his place. And, depend upon it, all work must be done at last, not in a disorderly, scrambling, doggish way, but in an ordered, soldierly, human way—a lawful way. Men are enlisted for the labour that kills—the labour of war: they are counted, trained, fed, dressed, and praised for that. Let them be enlisted also for the labour that feeds: let them be counted, trained, fed, dressed, praised for that. Teach the plough exercise as carefully as you do the sword exercise, and let the officers of troops of life be held as much gentlemen as the officers of troops of death; and all is done: but neither this, nor any other right thing, can be accomplished—you can't even see your way to it—unless, first of all, both servant and master are resolved that, come what will of it, they will do each other justice. People are perpetually squabbling about what will be best to do, or easiest to do, or adviseablest to do, or profitablest to do; but they never, so far as I hear them talk, ever ask what it is *just* to do. And it is the law of heaven that you shall not be able to judge what is wise or easy, unless you are first resolved to judge what is just, and to do it. That is the one thing constantly reiterated by our Master—the order of all others that is given oftenest—" Do justice and judgment." That's your Bible order; that's the " Service of God," not praying nor psalm-singing. You are told, indeed, to sing psalms when you are merry, and to pray when you need anything; and, by the perversion of the Evil Spirit, we get to think that praying and psalm-singing are " service." If a child finds itself in want of anything, it runs in and asks its father for it—does it call that, doing its father a service? If it begs for a toy or a piece of cake—does it call that serving its father? That, with God, is prayer, and He likes to hear it: He likes you to ask Him for cake when you want it; but He dosen't call that " serving Him." Begging is not serving: God likes mere beggars as little as you do—He likes honest servants, not beggars. So when a child loves its father very much, and is very happy, it may sing little songs about him; but it doesn't call that, serving its father; neither is singing songs about God, serving God. It is enjoying ourselves, if it's anything; most probably it is nothing: but if it's anything, it is serving ourselves, not God.   And yet we are impudent enough to call our beggings and chauntings " Divine Service: " we say, " Divine service will be ' performed ' " (that's our word —the form of it gone through) " at eleven o'clock." Alas!—unless we perform Divine service in every willing act of life, we never perform it at all.   The one Divine work—the one ordered sacrifice—is to do justice; and it is the last we are ever inclined to do.   Anything rather than that!   As much charity as you choose, but no justice.   " Nay," you will say, " charity is greater than justice."   Yes, it is greater; it is the summit of justice —it is the temple of which justice is the foundation. But you can't have the top without the bottom; you cannot build upon charity.   You must build upon justice, for this main reason, that you have not, at first, charity to build with.   It is the last reward of good work. Do justice to your brother (you can do that, whether you love him or not), and you will come to love him. But do injustice to him, because you don't love him; and you will come to hate him.   It is all very fine to think you can build upon charity to begin with; but you will find all you have got to begin with, begins at home, and is essentially love of yourself.   You well-to-do people, for instance, who are here to-night, will go to " Divine Service " next Sunday, all nice and tidy, and your little children will have their tight little Sunday boots on, and lovely little Sunday feathers in their hats; and you'll think, complacently and piously, how lovely they look!   So they do; and you love them heartily, and you like sticking feathers in their hats.   That's all right: that *is* charity; but it is charity beginning at home.   Then you will come to the poor little crossing-sweeper, got up also,—it, in its Sunday dress,—the dirtiest rags it has,—that it may beg the better: we shall give it a penny, and think how good we are. That's charity going abroad.   But what does Justice say, walking and watching near us?   Christian Justice has been strangely mute, and seemingly blind; and, if not blind, decrepit, this many a day: she keeps her accounts still, however—quite steadily—doing them at nights, carefully, with her bandage off, and through acutest spectacles (the only modern scientific invention she cares about).   You must put your ear down ever so close to her lips to hear her speak; and then you will start at what she first whispers, for it will certainly be, " Why shouldn't that little crossing-sweeper have a feather on its head, as well as your own child? " Then you may ask Justice, in an amazed manner, " How she can possibly be so foolish as to think children could sweep crossings with feathers on their heads? " Then you stoop again, and Justice says—still in her dull, stupid way—" Then, why don't you, every other Sunday, leave your child to sweep the crossing, and take the little sweeper to church in a hat and feather? " Mercy on us (you think), what will she say next?   And you answer, of course, that " you don't, because everybody ought to remain content in the position in which Providence has placed them."   Ah, my friends, that's the gist of the whole question.   *Did* Providence put them in that position, or did *you* ?   You knock a man into a ditch, and then you tell him to remain content in the " position in which Providence has placed him." That's modern Christianity.   You say—" *We* did not knock him into the ditch."   How do you know what you have done, or are doing?   That's just what we have all got to know, and what we shall never know, until the question with us, every morning, is, not how to do the gainful thing, but how to do the just thing; nor until we are at least so far on the way to being Christian, as to have understood that maxim of the poor half-way Mahometan, " One hour.in the execution of justice is worth seventy years of prayer."

Supposing, then, we have it determined with appropriate justice, *who* is to do the hand work, the next questions must be how the hand-workers are to be paid,

and how they are to be refreshed, and what play they are
to have. Now, the possible quantity of play depends
on the possible quantity of pay; and the quantity of
pay is not a matter for consideration to hand-workers
only, but to all workers. Generally, good, useful work,
whether of the hand or head, is either ill-paid, or not paid
at all. I don't say it should be so, but it always is so.
People, as a rule, only pay for being amused or being
cheated, not for being served. Five thousand a year to
your talker, and a shilling a day to your fighter, digger,
and thinker, is the rule. None of the best head work in
art, literature, or science, is ever paid for. How much
do you think Homer got for his *Iliad?* or Dante for his
Paradise? only bitter bread and salt, and going up and
down other people's stairs. In science, the man who
discovered the telescope, and first saw heaven, was paid
with a dungeon; the man who invented the microscope,
and first saw earth, died of starvation, driven from his
home: it is indeed very clear that God means all
thoroughly good work and talk to be done for nothing.
Baruch, the scribe, did not get a penny a line for writing
Jeremiah's second roll for him, I fancy; and St. Stephen
did not get bishop's pay for that long sermon of his
to the Pharisees; nothing but stones. For indeed that
is the world-father's proper payment. So surely as
any of the world's children work for the world's good,
honestly, with head and heart; and come to it, saying,
" Give us a little bread, just to keep the life in us," the
world-father answers them, " No, my children, not
bread; a stone, if you like, or as many as you need, to
keep you quiet." But the hand-workers are not so ill
off as all this comes to. The worst that can happen to
you is to break stones; not be broken by them. And
for you there will come a time for better payment; some
day, assuredly, more pence will be paid to Peter the
Fisherman, and fewer to Peter the Pope; we shall pay
people not quite so much for talking in Parliament and
doing nothing, as for holding their tongues out of it

and doing something; we shall pay our ploughman a little more, and our lawyer a little less, and so on: but, at least, we may even now take care that whatever work is done shall be fully paid for; and the man who does it paid for it, not somebody else; and that it shall be done in an orderly, soldierly, well-guided, wholesome way, under good captains and lieutenants of labour; and that it shall have its appointed times of rest, and enough of them; and that in those times the play shall be wholesome play, not in theatrical gardens, with tin flowers and gas sunshine, and girls dancing because of their misery; but in true gardens, with real flowers, and real sunshine, and children dancing because of their gladness; so that truly the streets shall be full (the "streets," mind you, not the gutters) of children, playing in the midst thereof. We may take care that working men shall have at least as good books to read as anybody else, when they've time to read them; and as comfortable firesides to sit at as anybody else, when they've time to sit at them. This, I think, can be managed for you, my working friends, in the good time.

IV. I must go on, however, to our last head, concerning ourselves all, as workers. What is wise work, and what is foolish work? What the difference between sense and nonsense, in daily occupation?

Well, wise work is, briefly, work *with* God. Foolish work is work *against* God. And work done with God, which He will help, may be briefly described as " Putting in Order "—that is, enforcing God's law of order, spiritual and material, over men and things. The first thing you have to do, essentially; the real " good work " is, with respect to men, to enforce justice, and with respect to things, to enforce tidiness, and fruitfulness. And against these two great human deeds, justice and order, there are perpetually two great demons contending,—the devil of iniquity, or inequity, and the devil of disorder, or of death; for death is only consummation of disorder. You have to fight these two fiends daily. So far as you don't fight against the fiend of iniquity, you work for him. You "work iniquity," and the judgment upon you, for all your "Lord, Lord's," will be "Depart from me, ye that work iniquity." And so far as you do not resist the fiend of disorder, you work disorder, and you yourself do the work of Death, which is sin, and has for its wages, Death himself.

Observe then, all wise work is mainly threefold in character. It is honest, useful, and cheerful.

I. It is HONEST. I hardly know anything more strange than that you recognise honesty in play, and you do not in work. In your lightest games, you have always some one to see what you call "fair-play." In boxing, you must hit fair; in racing, start fair. Your English watchword is fair-play, your English hatred, foul-play. Did it ever strike you that you wanted another watchword also, fair-work, and another hatred also, foul-work? Your prize-fighter has some honour in him yet; and so have the men in the ring round him: they will judge him to lose the match, by foul hitting. But your prize-merchant gains his match by foul selling, and no one cries out against that. You drive a gambler out of the gambling-room who loads dice, but you leave a tradesman in flourishing business, who loads scales! For observe, all dishonest dealing *is* loading scales. What does it matter whether I get short weight, adulterate substance, or dishonest fabric? The fault in the fabric is incomparably the worst of the two. Give me short measure of food, and I only lose by you; but give me adulterate food, and I die by you. Here, then, is your chief duty, you workmen and tradesmen, —to be true to yourselves, and to us who would help you. We can do nothing for you, nor you for yourselves, without honesty. Get that, you get all; without that, your suffrages, your reforms, your free-trade measures, your institutions of science, are all in vain. It is useless to put your heads together, if you can't put your hearts together. Shoulder to shoulder, right hand to right hand, among yourselves, and no wrong hand to anybody else, and you'll win the world yet.

II. Then, secondly, wise work is USEFUL. No man minds, or ought to mind, its being hard, if only it comes to something; but when it is hard, and comes to nothing; when all our bees' business turns to spiders'; and for honey-comb we have only resultant cobweb, blown away by the next breeze,—that is the cruel thing for the worker. Yet do we ever ask ourselves, personally, or even nationally, whether our work is coming to anything or not? We don't care to keep what has been nobly done; still less do we care to do nobly what others would keep; and, least of all, to make the work itself useful instead of deadly to the doer, so as to use his life indeed, but not to waste it. Of all wastes, the greatest waste that you can commit is the waste of labour. If you went down in the morning into your dairy, and you found that your youngest child had got down before you; and that he and the cat were at play together, and that he had poured out all the cream on the floor for the cat to lap up, you would scold the child, and be sorry the milk was wasted. But if, instead of wooden bowls with milk in them, there are golden bowls with human life in them, and instead of the cat to play with,—the devil to play with; and you yourself the player; and instead of leaving that golden bowl to be broken by God at the fountain, you break it in the dust yourself, and pour the human blood out on the ground for the fiend to lick up—that is no waste! What! you perhaps think, " to waste the labour of men is not to kill them." Is it not? I should like to know how you could kill them more utterly—kill them with second deaths, seventh deaths, hundredfold deaths? It is the slightest way of killing to stop a man's breath. Nay, the hunger, and the cold, and the little whistling bullets—our love-messengers between nation and nation,—have brought pleasant messages from us to many a man before now; orders of sweet release, and leave at last to go where he will be most welcome and most happy. At the worst you do but shorten his life, you do not corrupt his life. But if you put him to base labour, if you bind his thoughts, if you blind his eyes, if you blunt his hopes, if you steal his joys, if you stunt his body, and blast his soul, and at last leave him not so much as to reap the poor fruit of his degradation, but gather that for yourself, and dismiss him to the grave, when you have done with him, having, so far as in you lay, made the walls of that grave everlasting: (though, indeed, I fancy the goodly bricks of some of our family vaults will hold closer in the resurrection day than the sod over the labourer's head), this you think is no waste, and no sin!

III. Then, lastly, wise work is CHEERFUL, as a child's work is. And now I want you to take one thought home with you, and let it stay with you.

Everybody in this room has been taught to pray daily, " Thy kingdom come." Now, if we hear a man swear in the streets, we think it very wrong, and say he " takes God's name in vain." But there's a twenty times worse way of taking His name in vain, than that. It is to *ask God for what we don't want.* He doesn't like that sort of prayer. If you don't want a thing, don't ask for it: such asking is the worst mockery of your King you can mock Him with; the soldiers striking Him on the head with the reed was nothing to that. If you do not wish for His kingdom, don't pray for it. But if you do, you must do more than pray for it; you must work for it. And, to work for it, you must know what it is: we have all prayed for it many a day without thinking. Observe, it is a kingdom that is to come to us; we are not to go to it. Also, it is not to be a king-dom of the dead, but of the living. Also, it is not to come all at once, but quietly; nobody knows how. " The kingdom of God cometh not with observation." Also, it is not to come outside of us, but in the hearts of us: " the kingdom of God is within you." And, being within us, it is not a thing to be seen, but to be felt; and though it brings all substance of good with it, it does not consist in that: " the kingdom of God is not meat and drink, but righteousness, peace, and joy in the Holy Ghost: " joy, that is to say, in the holy, healthful, and helpful Spirit. Now, if we want to work for this kingdom, and to bring it, and enter into it, there's just one condition to be first accepted. You must enter it as children, or not at all: " Whosoever will not receive it as a little child shall not enter therein." And again, " Suffer little children to come unto me, and forbid them not, for of such is the kingdom of heaven."

Of such, observe. Not of children themselves, but of such as children. I believe most mothers who read that text think that all heaven is to be full of babies. But that's not so. There will be children there, but the hoary head is the crown. " Length of days, and long life and peace," that is the blessing, not to die in babyhood. Children die but for their parents' sins; God means them to live, but He can't let them always; then they have their earlier place in heaven: and the little child of David, vainly prayed for;—the little child of Jeroboam, killed by its mother's step on its own threshold,—they will be there. But weary old David, and weary old Barzillai, having learned children's lessons at last, will be there too: and the one question for us all, young or old, is, have we learned our child's lesson? it is the *character* of children we want, and must gain at our peril; let us see, briefly, in what it consists.

The first character of right childhood is that it is Modest. A well-bred child does not think it can teach its parents, or that it knows everything. It may think its father and mother know everything,—perhaps that all grown-up people know everything; very certainly it is sure that *it* does not. And it is always asking questions, and wanting to know more. Well, that is

the first character of a good and wise man at his work.
To know that he knows very little;—to perceive that
there are many above him wiser than he; and to be
always asking questions, wanting to learn, not to teach.
No one ever teaches well who wants to teach, or governs
well who wants to govern; it is an old saying (Plato's,
but I know not if his, first), and as wise as old.

Then, the second character of right childhood is to
be Faithful. Perceiving that its father knows best
what is good for it, and having found always, when it
has tried its own way against his, that he was right
and it was wrong, a noble child trusts him at last wholly,
gives him its hand, and will walk blindfold with him,
if he bids it. And that is the true character of all good
men also, as obedient workers, or soldiers under captains.
They must trust their captains;—they are bound for
their lives to choose none but those whom they *can*
trust. Then, they are not always to be thinking that
what seems strange to them, or wrong in what they
are desired to do, *is* strange or wrong. They know
their captain: where he leads they must follow, what
he bids they must do; and without this trust and
faith, without this captainship and soldiership, no
great deed, no great salvation, is possible to man.
Among all the nations it is only when this faith is
attained by them that they become great: the Jew,
the Greek, and the Mahometan, agree at least in testify-
ing to this. It was a deed of this absolute trust which
made Abraham the father of the faithful; it was the
declaration of the power of God as captain over all men,
and the acceptance of a leader appointed by Him as
commander of the faithful, which laid the foundation
of whatever national power yet exists in the East;
and the deed of the Greeks, which has become the type
of unselfish and noble soldiership to all lands, and to
all times, was commemorated, on the tomb of those
who gave their lives to do it, in the most pathetic, so
far as I know, or can feel, of all human utterances:

" Oh, stranger, go and tell our people that we are lying here, having *obeyed* their words."

Then, the third character of right childhood is to be Loving and Generous. Give a little love to a child, and you get a great deal back. It loves everything near it, when it is a right kind of child—would hurt nothing, would give the best it has away, always, if you need it—does not lay plans for getting everything in the house for itself, and delights in helping people; you cannot please it so much as by giving it a chance of being useful, in ever so little a way.

And because of all these characters, lastly, it is Cheerful. Putting its trust in its father, it is careful for nothing—being full of love to every creature, it is happy always, whether in its play or its duty. Well, that's the great worker's character also. Taking no thought for the morrow; taking thought only for the duty of the day; trusting somebody else to take care of to-morrow; knowing indeed what labour is, but not what sorrow is; and always ready for play—beautiful play,—for lovely human play is like the play of the Sun. There's a worker for you. He, steady to his time, is set as a strong man to run his course, but also, he *rejoiceth* as a strong man to run his course. See how he plays in the morning, with the mists below, and the clouds above, with a ray here and a flash there, and a shower of jewels everywhere; — that's the Sun's play; and great human play is like his—all various—all full of light and life, and tender, as the dew of the morning.

So then, you have the child's character in these four things—Humility, Faith, Charity, and Cheerfulness. That's what you have got to be converted to. " Except ye be converted and become as little children "—You hear much of conversion now-a-days; but people always seem to think they have got to be made wretched by conversion,—to be converted to long faces. No, friends, you have got to be converted to short ones; you have to repent into childhood, to repent into delight, and delightsomeness. You can't go into a conventicle but you'll hear plenty of talk of backsliding. Backsliding, indeed! I can tell you, on the ways most of us go, the faster we slide back the better. Slide back into the cradle, if going on is into the grave—back, I tell you; back—out of your long faces, and into your long clothes. It is among children only, and as children only, that you will find medicine for your healing and true wisdom for your teaching. There is poison in the counsels of the *men* of this world; the words they speak are all bitterness, " the poison of asps is under their lips," but " the sucking child shall play by the hole of the asp." There is death in the looks of men. " Their eyes are privily set against the poor; " they are as the uncharmable serpent, the cockatrice, which slew by seeing. But " the weaned child shall lay his hand on the cockatrice den." There is death in the steps of men: " their feet are swift to shed blood; they have compassed us in our steps like the lion that is greedy of his prey, and the young lion lurking in secret places," but, in that kingdom, the wolf shall lie down with the lamb, and the fatling with the lion, and " a little child shall lead them." There is death in the thoughts of men: the world is one wide riddle to them, darker and darker as it draws to a close; but the secret of it is known to the child, and the Lord of heaven and earth is most to be thanked in that " He has hidden these things from the wise and prudent, and has revealed them unto babes." Yes, and there is death—infinitude of death in the principalities and powers of men. As far as the east is from the west, so far our sins are—*not* set from us, but multiplied around us: the Sun himself, think you he *now* " rejoices " to run his course, when he plunges westward to the horizon, so widely red, not with clouds, but blood? And it will be red more widely yet. Whatever drought of the early and latter rain may be, there will be none of that red rain. You fortify yourselves, you arm yourselves against it in vain; the enemy and avenger will be upon you also, unless you learn that it is not out of the mouths of the knitted gun, or the smoothed rifle, but " out of the mouths of babes and sucklings " that the strength is ordained. which shall " still the enemy and avenger."

LECTURE II

TRAFFIC

D

LECTURE II

TRADE

LECTURE II

(Delivered in the Town Hall, Bradford.)

My good Yorkshire friends, you asked me down here among your hills that I might talk to you about this Exchange you are going to build: but earnestly and seriously asking you to pardon me, I am going to do nothing of the kind. I cannot talk, or at least can say very little, about this same Exchange. I must talk of quite other things, though not willingly;—I could not deserve your pardon, if, when you invited me to speak on one subject, I wilfully spoke on another. But I cannot speak, to purpose, of anything about which I do not care; and most simply and sorrowfully I have to tell you, in the outset, that I do *not* care about this Exchange of yours.

If, however, when you sent me your invitation, I had answered, " I won't come, I don't care about the Exchange of Bradford," you would have been justly offended with me, not knowing the reasons of so blunt a carelessness. So I have come down, hoping that you will patiently let me tell you why, on this, and many other such occasions, I now remain silent, when formerly I should have caught at the opportunity of speaking to a gracious audience.

In a word, then, I do not care about this Exchange, —because *you* don't; and because you know perfectly well I cannot make you. Look at the essential circum-

51

stances of the case, which you, as business men, know perfectly well, though perhaps you think I forget them. You are going to spend £30,000, which to you, collectively, is nothing; the buying a new coat is, as to the cost of it, a much more important matter of consideration to me than building a new Exchange is to you. But you think you may as well have the right thing for your money. You know there are a great many odd styles of architecture about; you don't want to do anything ridiculous; you hear of me, among others, as a respectable architectural man-milliner: and you send for me, that I may tell you the leading fashion; and what is, in our shops, for the moment, the newest and sweetest thing in pinnacles.

Now, pardon me for telling you frankly, you cannot have good architecture merely by asking people's advice on occasion. All good architecture is the expression of national life and character; and it is produced by a prevalent and eager national taste, or desire for beauty. And I want you to think a little of the deep significance of this word " taste; " for no statement of mine has been more earnestly or oftener controverted than that good taste is essentially a moral quality. " No," say many of my antagonists, " taste is one thing, morality is another. Tell us what is pretty: we shall be glad to know that: but preach no sermons to us."

Permit me, therefore, to fortify this old dogma of mine somewhat. Taste is not only a part and an index of morality;—it is the ONLY morality. The first, and last, and closest trial question to any living creature is, " What do you like? " Tell me what you like, and I'll tell you what you are. Go out into the street, and ask the first man or woman you meet, what their " taste " is; and if they answer candidly, you know them, body and soul. " You, my friend in the rags, with the unsteady gait, what do *you* like? " " A pipe, and a quartern of gin." I know you. " You, good woman, with the quick step and tidy bonnet, what do you like?" "A swept hearth, and a clean tea-table; and my husband opposite me, and a baby at my breast." Good, I know you also. "You, little girl with the golden hair and the soft eyes, what do you like?" "My canary, and a run among the wood hyacinths." "You, little boy with the dirty hands, and the low forehead, what do you like?" "A shy at the sparrows, and a game at pitch-farthing." Good; we know them all now. What more need we ask?

"Nay," perhaps you answer; "we need rather to ask what these people and children do, than what they like. If they *do* right, it is no matter that they like what is wrong; and if they *do* wrong, it is no matter that they like what is right. Doing is the great thing; and it does not matter that the man likes drinking, so that he does not drink; nor that the little girl likes to be kind to her canary, if she will not learn her lessons; nor that the little boy likes throwing stones at the sparrows, if he goes to the Sunday school." Indeed, for a short time, and in a provisional sense, this is true. For if, resolutely, people do what is right, in time they come to like doing it. But they only are in a right moral state when they *have* come to like doing it; and as long as they don't like it, they are still in a vicious state. The man is not in health of body who is always thirsting for the bottle in the cupboard, though he bravely bears his thirst; but the man who heartily enjoys water in the morning and wine in the evening, each in its proper quantity and time. And the entire object of true education is to make people not merely *do* the right things, but *enjoy* the right things—not merely industrious, but to love industry—not merely learned, but to love knowledge—not merely pure, but to love purity—not merely just, but to hunger and thirst after justice.

But you may answer or think, "Is the liking for outside ornaments,—for pictures, or statues, or furniture, or architecture,—a moral quality?" Yes, most surely, if a rightly set liking. Taste for *any* pictures or statues is not a moral quality, but taste for good ones is. Only here again we have to define the word " good." I don't mean by " good," clever—or learned—or difficult in the doing. Take a picture by Teniers, of sots quarrelling over their dice; it is an entirely clever picture; so clever that nothing in its kind has ever been done equal to it; but it is also an entirely base and evil picture. It is an expression of delight in the prolonged contemplation of a vile thing, and delight in that is an " unmannered," or " immoral " quality. It is " bad taste " in the profoundest sense—it is the taste of the devils. On the other hand, a picture of Titian's, or a Greek statue, or a Greek coin, or a Turner landscape, expresses delight in the perpetual contemplation of a good and perfect thing. That is an entirely moral quality—it is the taste of the angels. And all delight in art, and all love of it, resolve themselves into simple love of that which deserves love. That deserving is the quality which we call " loveliness "—(we ought to have an opposite word, hateliness, to be said of the things which deserve to be hated); and it is not an indifferent nor optional thing whether we love this or that; but it is just the vital function of all our being. What we *like* determines what we *are*, and is the sign of what we are; and to teach taste is inevitably to form character. As I was thinking over this, in walking up Fleet Street the other day, my eye caught the title of a book standing open in a bookseller's window. It was—*On the Necessity of the Diffusion of Taste among all Classes*. " Ah," I thought to myself, " my classifying friend, when you have diffused your taste, where will your classes be? The man who likes what you like, belongs to the same class with you, I think. Inevitably so. You may put him to other work if you choose; but, by the condition you have brought him into, he will dislike the other work as much as you would yourself. You get hold of a scavenger, or a costermonger, who enjoyed the *Newgate Calendar* for literature, and " Pop goes the Weasel " for music. You think you can make him like Dante and Beethoven? I wish you joy of your lessons; but if you do, you have made a gentleman of him:—he won't like to go back to his costermongering."

And so completely and unexceptionally is this so, that, if I had time to-night, I could show you that a nation cannot be affected by any vice, or weakness, without expressing it, legibly, and for ever, either in bad art, or by want of art; and that there is no national virtue, small or great, which is not manifestly expressed in all the art which circumstances enable the people possessing that virtue to produce. Take, for instance, your great English virtue of enduring and patient courage. You have at present in England only one art of any consequence—that is, iron-working. You know thoroughly well how to cast and hammer iron. Now, do you think in those masses of lava which you build volcanic cones to melt, and which you forge at the mouths of the Infernos you have created; do you think, on those iron plates, your courage and endurance are not written for ever—not merely with an iron pen, but on iron parchment? And take also your great English vice—European vice—vice of all the world—vice of all other worlds that roll or shine in heaven, bearing with them yet the atmosphere of hell—the vice of jealousy, which brings competition into your commerce, treachery into your councils, and dishonour into your wars—that vice which has rendered for you, and for your next neighbouring nation, the daily occupations of existence no longer possible, but with the mail upon your breasts and the sword loose in its sheath; so that, at last, you have realised for all the multitudes of the two great peoples who lead the so-called civilisation of the earth,—you have realised for them all, I say, in

person and in policy, what was once true only of the
rough Border riders of your Cheviot hills—

> " They carved at the meal
> With gloves of steel,
> And they drank the red wine through the helmet barr'd; "—

do you think that this national shame and dastardliness
of heart are not written as legibly on every rivet of your
iron armour as the strength of the right hands that
forged it?   Friends, I know not whether this thing be
the more ludicrous or the more melancholy.   It is quite
unspeakably both.   Suppose, instead of being now sent
for by you, I had been sent for by some private gentleman, living in a suburban house, with his garden separated only by a fruit-wall from his next door neighbour's;
and he had called me to consult with him on the furnish-
ing of his drawing-room.   I begin looking about me,
and find the walls rather bare; I think such and such
a paper might be desirable—perhaps a little fresco here
and there on the ceiling—a damask curtain or so at the
windows.   " Ah," says my employer, "damask curtains,
indeed!   That's all very fine, but you know I can't
afford that kind of thing just now!"   " Yet the world
credits you with a splendid income!"   " Ah, yes,"
says my friend, " but do you know, at present, I am
obliged to spend it nearly all in steel-traps?"   " Steel-
traps! for whom?"   " Why, for that fellow on the
other side the wall, you know: we're very good friends,
capital friends; but we are obliged to keep our traps
set on both sides of the wall; we could not possibly
keep on friendly terms without them, and our spring
guns.   The worst of it is, we are both clever fellows
enough; and there's never a day passes that we don't
find out a new trap, or a new gun-barrel, or something;
we spend about fifteen millions a year each in our traps,
take it altogether; and I don't see how we're to do with
less."   A highly comic state of life for two private
gentlemen!   but for two nations, it seems to me, not

wholly comic? Bedlam would be comic, perhaps, if there were only one madman in it; and your Christmas pantomime is comic, when there is only one clown in it; but when the whole world turns clown, and paints itself red with its own heart's blood instead of vermilion, it is something else than comic, I think.

Mind, I know a great deal of this is play, and willingly allow for that. You don't know what to do with yourselves for a sensation: fox-hunting and cricketing will not carry you through the whole of this unendurably long mortal life: you liked pop-guns when you were schoolboys, and rifles and Armstrongs are only the same things better made: but then the worst of it is, that what was play to you when boys, was not play to the sparrows; and what is play to you now, is not play to the small birds of State neither; and for the black eagles, you are somewhat shy of taking shots at them, if I mistake not.

I must get back to the matter in hand, however. Believe me, without farther instance, I could show you, in all time, that every nation's vice, or virtue, was written in its art: the soldiership of early Greece; the sensuality of late Italy; the visionary religion of Tuscany; the splendid human energy and beauty of Venice. I have no time to do this to-night (I have done it elsewhere before now); but I proceed to apply the principle to ourselves in a more searching manner.

I notice that among all the new buildings which cover your once wild hills, churches and schools are mixed in due, that is to say, in large proportion, with your mills and mansions; and I notice also that the churches and schools are almost always Gothic, and the mansions and mills are never Gothic. Will you allow me to ask precisely the meaning of this? For, remember, it is peculiarly a modern phenomenon. When Gothic was invented, houses were Gothic as well as churches; and when the Italian style superseded the Gothic, churches were Italian as well as houses. If there is a Gothic spire to the cathedral of Antwerp, there is a Gothic belfry to the Hôtel de Ville at Brussels; if Inigo Jones builds an Italian Whitehall, Sir Christopher Wren builds an Italian St. Paul's. But now you live under one school of architecture, and worship under another. What do you mean by doing this? Am I to understand that you are thinking of changing your architecture back to Gothic; and that you treat your churches experimentally, because it does not matter what mistakes you make in a church? Or am I to understand that you consider Gothic a pre-eminently sacred and beautiful mode of building, which you think, like the fine frankincense, should be mixed for the tabernacle only, and reserved for your religious services? For if this be the feeling, though it may seem at first as if it were graceful and reverent, you will find that, at the root of the matter, it signifies neither more nor less than that you have separated your religion from your life.

For consider what a wide significance this fact has; and remember that it is not you only, but all the people of England, who are behaving thus just now.

You have all got into the habit of calling the church " the house of God." I have seen, over the doors of many churches, the legend actually carved, " *This* is the house of God, and this is the gate of heaven." Now, note where that legend comes from, and of what place it was first spoken. A boy leaves his father's house to go on a long journey on foot, to visit his uncle: he has to cross a wild hill-desert; just as if one of your own boys had to cross the wolds of Westmoreland, to visit an uncle at Carlisle. The second or third day your boy finds himself somewhere between Hawes and Brough, in the midst of the moors, at sunset. It is stony ground, and boggy; he cannot go one foot farther that night. Down he lies, to sleep, on Wharnside, where best he may, gathering a few of the stones together to put under his head;—so wild the place is, he cannot get anything but stones. And there, lying under the broad night, he has a dream; and he sees a ladder set up on the earth, and the top of it reaches to heaven, and the angels of God are ascending and descending upon it. And when he wakes out of his sleep, he says, " How dreadful is this place; surely, this is none other than the house of God, and this is the gate of heaven." This PLACE, observe; not this church; not this city; not this stone, even, which he puts up for a memorial—the piece of flint on which his head has lain. But this *place ;* this windy slope of Wharnside; this moorland hollow, torrent-bitten, snow-blighted; this *any* place where God lets down the ladder. And how are you to know where that will be? or how are you to determine where it may be, but by being ready for it always? Do you know where the lightning is to fall next? You *do* know that, partly; you can guide the lightning; but you cannot guide the going forth of the Spirit, which is as that lightning when it shines from the east to the west.

But the perpetual and insolent warping of that strong verse to serve a merely ecclesiastical purpose, is only one of the thousand instances in which we sink back into gross Judaism. We call our churches " temples." Now, you know, or ought to know, they are *not* temples. They have never had, never can have, anything whatever to do with temples. They are " synagogues "— " gathering places "—where you gather yourselves together as an assembly; and by not calling them so, you again miss the force of another mighty text— " Thou, when thou prayest, shalt not be as the hypocrites are; for they love to pray standing in the *churches* " [we should translate it], " that they may be seen of men. But thou, when thou prayest, enter into thy closet, and when thou hast shut thy door, pray to thy Father,"—which is, not in chancel nor in aisle, but " in secret."

Now, you feel, as I say this to you—I know you feel— as if I were trying to take away the honour of your churches. Not so; I am trying to prove to you the honour of your houses and your hills; I am trying to show you—not that the Church is not sacred—but that the whole Earth is. I would have you feel, what careless, what constant, with infectious sin there is in all modes of thought, whereby, in calling your churches only " holy," you call your hearths and homes profane; and have separated yourselves from the heathen by casting all your household gods to the ground, instead of recognising, in the places of their many and feeble Lares, the presence of your One and Mighty Lord and Lar.

" But what has all this to do with our Exchange? " you ask me, impatiently. My dear friends, it has just everything to do with it; on these inner and great questions depend all the outer and little ones; and if you have asked me down here to speak to you, because you had before been interested in anything I have written, you must know that all I have yet said about architecture was to show this. The book I called *The Seven Lamps* was to show that certain right states of temper and moral feeling were the magic powers by which all good architecture, without exception, had been produced. *The Stones of Venice* had, from beginning to end, no other aim than to show that the Gothic architecture of Venice had arisen out of, and indicated in all its features, a state of pure national faith, and of domestic virtue; and that its Renaissance architecture had arisen out of, and in all its features indicated, a state of concealed national infidelity, and of domestic corruption. And now, you ask me what style is best to build in; and how can I answer, knowing the meaning of the two styles, but by another question—do you mean to build as Christians or as Infidels? And still more—do you mean to build as honest Christians or as honest Infidels? as thoroughly and confessedly either one or the other? You don't like to be asked such rude questions. I cannot help it; they are of much more importance than this Exchange business; and if they can be at once answered, the Exchange business settles itself in a moment.   But, before I press them farther, I must ask leave to explain one point clearly.   In all my past work, my endeavour has been to show that good architecture is essentially religious—the production of a faithful and virtuous, not of an infidel and corrupted people.   But in the course of doing this, I have had also to show that good architecture is not *ecclesiastical*. People are so apt to look upon religion as the business of the clergy, not their own, that the moment they hear of anything depending on " religion," they think it must also have depended on the priesthood; and I have had to take what place was to be occupied between these two errors, and fight both, often with seeming contradiction.   Good architecture is the work of good and believing men; therefore, you say, at least some people say, " Good architecture must essentially have been the work of the clergy, not of the laity."   No—a thousand times no; good architecture has always been the work of the commonalty, *not* of the clergy.   What, you say, those glorious cathedrals—the pride of Europe—did their builders not form Gothic architecture?   No; they corrupted Gothic architecture.   Gothic was formed in the baron's castle, and the burgher's street.   It was formed by the thoughts, and hands, and powers of free citizens and soldier kings.   By the monk it was used as an instrument for the aid of his superstition: when that superstition became a beautiful madness, and the best hearts of Europe vainly dreamed and pined in the cloister, and vainly raged and perished in the crusade,—through that fury of perverted faith and wasted war, the Gothic rose also to its loveliest, most fantastic, and finally, most foolish dreams; and, in those dreams, was lost.

I hope, now, that there is no risk of your misunderstanding me when I come to the gist of what I want to say to-night;—when I repeat, that every great

national architecture has been the result and exponent
of a great national religion. You can't have bits of it
here, bits there—you must have it everywhere or nowhere. It is not the monopoly of a clerical company—
it is not the exponent of a theological dogma—it is not
the hieroglyphic writing of an initiated priesthood;
it is the manly language of a people inspired by resolute
and common purpose, and rendering resolute and
common fidelity to the legible laws of an undoubted
God.

Now there have as yet been three distinct schools
of European architecture. I say, European, because
Asiatic and African architectures belong so entirely to
other races and climates, that there is no question of
them here; only, in passing, I will simply assure you
that whatever is good or great in Egypt, and Syria,
and India, is just good or great for the same reasons
as the buildings on our side of the Bosphorus. We
Europeans, then, have had three great religions: the
Greek, which was the worship of the God of Wisdom
and Power; the Mediæval, which was the worship of
the God of Judgment and Consolation; the Renaissance,
which was the worship of the God of Pride and Beauty:
these three we have had—they are past,—and now, at
last, we English have got a fourth religion, and a God
of our own, about which I want to ask you. But I
must explain these three old ones first.

I repeat, first, the Greeks essentially worshipped the
God of Wisdom; so that whatever contended against
their religion,—to the Jews a stumbling-block,—was,
to the Greeks—*Foolishness*.

The first Greek idea of deity was that expressed in
the word, of which we keep the remnant in our words
" *Di*-urnal " and " *Di*-vine "—the god of *Day*, Jupiter
the revealer. Athena is his daughter, but especially
daughter of the Intellect, springing armed from the
head. We are only with the help of recent investigation beginning to penetrate the depth of meaning

couched under the Athenaic symbols: but I may note rapidly, that her ægis, the mantle with the serpent fringes, in which she often, in the best statues, is represented as folding up her left hand for better guard, and the Gorgon on her shield, are both representative mainly of the chilling horror and sadness, (turning men to stone, as it were,) of the outmost and superficial spheres of knowledge—that knowledge which separates, in bitterness, hardness, and sorrow, the heart of the full-grown man from the heart of the child. For out of imperfect knowledge spring terror, dissension, danger, and disdain; but from perfect knowledge, given by the full-revealed Athena, strength and peace, in sign of which she is crowned with the olive spray, and bears the resistless spear.

This, then, was the Greek conception of purest Deity, and every habit of life, and every form of his art developed themselves from the seeking this bright, serene, resistless wisdom; and setting himself, as a man, to do things evermore rightly and strongly; [1] not with any ardent affection or ultimate hope; but with a resolute and continent energy of will, as knowing that for failure there was no consolation, and for sin there was no remission. And the Greek architecture rose unerring, bright, clearly defined, and self-contained.

Next followed in Europe the great Christian faith, which was essentially the religion of Comfort. Its great doctrine is the remission of sins; for which cause it happens, too often, in certain phases of Christianity,

[1] It is an error to suppose that the Greek worship, or seeking, was chiefly of Beauty. It was essentially of Rightness and Strength, founded on Forethought: the principal character of Greek art is not beauty, but Design: and the Dorian Apollo-worship and Athenian Virgin-worship are both expressions of adoration of divine Wisdom and Purity. Next to these great deities rank, in power over the national mind, Dionysus and Ceres, the givers of human strength and life; then, for heroic example, Hercules. There is no Venus-worship among the Greeks in the great times: and the Muses are essentially teachers of truth, and of its harmonies.

that sin and sickness themselves are partly glorified, as if, the more you had to be healed of, the more divine was the healing. The practical result of this doctrine, in art, is a continual contemplation of sin and disease, and of imaginary states of purification from them; thus we have an architecture conceived in a mingled sentiment of melancholy and aspiration, partly severe, partly luxuriant, which will bend itself to every one of our needs, and every one of our fancies, and be strong or weak with us, as we are strong or weak ourselves. It is, of all architecture, the basest, when base people build it—of all, the noblest, when built by the noble.

And now note that both these religions—Greek and Mediæval—perished by falsehood in their own main purpose. The Greek religion of Wisdom perished in a false philosophy—" Oppositions of science, falsely so called." The Mediæval religion of Consolation perished in false comfort; in remission of sins given lyingly. It was the selling of absolution that ended the Mediæval faith; and I can tell you more, it is the selling of absolution which, to the end of time, will mark false Christianity. Pure Christianity gives her remission of sins only by *ending* them; but false Christianity gets her remission of sins by *compounding for* them. And there are many ways of compounding for them. We English have beautiful little quiet ways of buying absolution, whether in low Church or high, far more cunning than any of Tetzel's trading.

Then, thirdly, there followed the religion of Pleasure, in which all Europe gave itself to luxury, ending in death. First, *bals masqués* in every saloon, and then guillotines in every square. And all these three worships issue in vast temple building. Your Greek worshipped Wisdom, and built you the Parthenon— the Virgin's temple. The Mediæval worshipped Consolation, and built you Virgin temples also—but to our Lady of Salvation. Then the Revivalist worshipped beauty, of a sort, and built you Versailles, and the

Vatican. Now, lastly, will you tell me what *we* worship, and what *we* build?

You know we are speaking always of the real, active, continual, national worship; that by which men act while they live; not that which they talk of when they die. Now, we have, indeed, a nominal religion, to which we pay tithes of property and sevenths of time; but we have also a practical and earnest religion, to which we devote nine-tenths of our property and six-sevenths of our time. And we dispute a great deal about the nominal religion; but we are all unanimous about this practical one, of which I think you will admit that the ruling goddess may be best generally described as the " Goddess of Getting-on," or " Britannia of the Market." The Athenians had an " Athena Agoraia," or Minerva of the Market; but she was a subordinate type of their goddess, while our Britannia Agoraia is the principal type of ours. And all your great architectural works are, of course, built to her. It is long since you built a great cathedral; and how you would laugh at me, if I proposed building a cathedral on the top of one of these hills of yours, taking it for an Acropolis! But your railroad mounds, prolonged masses of Acropolis; your railroad stations, vaster than the Parthenon, and innumerable; your chimneys, how much more mighty and costly than cathedral spires! your harbour-piers; your warehouses; your exchanges! —all these are built to your great Goddess of " Getting-on; " and she has formed, and will continue to form, your architecture, as long as you worship her; and it is quite vain to ask me to tell you how to build to *her;* you know far better than I.

There might, indeed, on some theories, be a conceivably good architecture for Exchanges—that is to say if there were any heroism in the fact or deed of exchange, which might be typically carved on the outside of your building. For, you know, all beautiful architecture must be adorned with sculpture or paint-

E

ing; and for sculpture or painting, you must have a subject. And hitherto it has been a received opinion among the nations of the world that the only right subjects for either, were *heroisms* of some sort. Even on his pots and his flagons, the Greek put a Hercules slaying lions, or an Apollo slaying serpents, or Bacchus slaying melancholy giants, and earthborn despondencies. On his temples, the Greek put contests of great warriors in founding states, or of gods with evil spirits. On his houses and temples alike, the Christian put carvings of angels conquering devils; or of hero-martyrs exchanging this world for another; subject inappropriate, I think, to our manner of exchange here. And the Master of Christians not only left his followers without any orders as to the sculpture of affairs of exchange on the outside of buildings, but gave some strong evidence of his dislike of affairs of exchange within them. And yet there might surely be a heroism in such affairs; and all commerce become a kind of selling of doves, not impious. The wonder has always been great to me, that heroism has never been supposed to be in anywise consistent with the practice of supplying people with food, or clothes; but rather with that of quartering oneself upon them for food, and stripping them of their clothes. Spoiling of armour is an heroic deed in all ages; but the selling of clothes, old, or new, has never taken any colour of magnanimity. Yet one does not see why feeding the hungry and clothing the naked should ever become base businesses, even when engaged in on a large scale. If one could contrive to attach the notion of conquest to them anyhow? so that, supposing there were anywhere an obstinate race, who refused to be comforted, one might take some pride in giving them compulsory comfort; and as it were, " occupying a country " with one's gifts, instead of one's armies? If one could only consider it as much a victory to get a barren field sown, as to get an eared field stripped; and contend who should build villages,

instead of who should " carry " them. Are not all
forms of heroism, conceivable in doing these serviceable deeds? You doubt who is strongest? It might
be ascertained by push of spade, as well as push of
sword. Who is wisest? There are witty things to be
thought of in planning other business than campaigns.
Who is bravest? There are always the elements to
fight with, stronger than men; and nearly as merciless.
The only absolutely and unapproachably heroic element
in the soldier's work seems to be—that he is paid little
for it—and regularly: while you traffickers, and ex-
changers, and others occupied in presumably benevolent
business, like to be paid much for it—and by chance.
I never can make out how it is that a knight-errant
does not expect to be paid for his trouble, but a pedlar-
errant always does;—that people are willing to take
hard knocks for nothing, but never to sell ribands
cheap;—that they are ready to go on fervent crusades
to recover the tomb of a buried God, never on any
travels to fulfil the orders of a living God;—that they
will go anywhere barefoot to preach their faith, but
must be well bribed to practise it, and are perfectly
ready to give the Gospel gratis, but never the loaves
and fishes. If you chose to take the matter up on any
such soldierly principle, to do your commerce, and your
feeding of nations, for fixed salaries; and to be as
particular about giving people the best food, and the
best cloth, as soldiers are about giving them the best
gunpowder, I could carve something for you on your
exchange worth looking at. But I can only at present
suggest decorating its frieze with pendant purses; and
making its pillars broad at the base, for the sticking
of bills. And in the innermost chambers of it there
might be a statue of Britannia of the Market, who may
have, perhaps advisably, a partridge for her crest,
typical at once of her courage in fighting for noble
ideas; and of her interest in game; and round its neck
the inscription in golden letters, " Perdix fovit quæ

non peperit."[1] Then, for her spear, she might have
a weaver's beam; and on her shield, instead of her
Cross, the Milanese boar, semi-fleeced, with the town
of Gennesaret proper, in the field and the legend, " In
the best market," and her corslet, of leather, folded
over her heart in the shape of a purse, with thirty slits
in it for a piece of money to go in at, on each day of the
month.   And I doubt not but that people would come
to see your exchange, and its goddess, with applause.

Nevertheless, I want to point out to you certain
strange characters in this goddess of yours. She
differs from the great Greek and Mediæval deities
essentially in two things—first, as to the continuance
of her presumed power; secondly, as to the extent
of it.

1st, as to the Continuance.

The Greek Goddess of Wisdom gave continual increase of wisdom, as the Christian Spirit of Comfort
(or Comforter) continual increase of comfort. There
was no question, with these, of any limit or cessation
of function. But with your Agora Goddess, that is
just the most important question. Getting on—but
where to? Gathering together—but how much? Do
you mean to gather always—never to spend? If so, I
wish you joy of your goddess, for I am just as well-off
as you, without the trouble of worshipping her at all.
But if you do not spend, somebody else will—somebody
else must.   And it is because of this (among many other
such errors) that I have fearlessly declared your so-
called science of Political Economy to be no science;
because, namely, it has omitted the study of exactly
the most important branch of the business—the study
of *spending*. For spend you must, and as much as you
make, ultimately.   You gather corn:—will you bury

[1] Jerem. xvii. 11 (best in Septuagint and Vulgate).   " As the
partridge, fostering what she brought not forth, so he that getteth
riches, not by right, shall leave them in the midst of his days, and
at his end shall be a fool."

England under a heap of grain; or will you, when you
have gathered, finally eat? You gather gold:—will
you make your house-roofs of it, or pave your streets
with it? That is still one way of spending it. But if
you keep it, that you may get more, I'll give you more;
I'll give you all the gold you want—all you can imagine
—if you can tell me what you'll do with it. You shall
have thousands of gold pieces;—thousands of thousands
—millions—mountains, of gold: where will you keep
them? Will you put an Olympus of silver upon a golden
Pelion—make Ossa like a wart? Do you think the
rain and dew would then come down to you, in the
streams from such mountains, more blessedly than they
will down the mountains which God has made for you,
of moss and whinstone? But it is not gold that you
want to gather! What is it? greenbacks? No; not
those neither. What is it then—is it ciphers after a
capital I? Cannot you practise writing ciphers, and
write as many as you want? Write ciphers for an
hour every morning, in a big book, and say every evening, I am worth all those noughts more than I was
yesterday. Won't that do? Well, what in the name
of Plutus is it you want? Not gold, not greenbacks,
not ciphers after a capital I? You will have to answer,
after all, " No; we want, somehow or other, money's
worth." Well, what is that? Let your Goddess of
Getting-on discover it, and let her learn to stay therein.

II. But there is yet another question to be asked
respecting this Goddess of Getting-on. The first was
of the continuance of her power; the second is of its
extent.

Pallas and the Madonna were supposed to be all the
world's Pallas, and all the world's Madonna. They
could teach all men, and they could comfort all men.
But, look strictly into the nature of the power of your
Goddess of Getting-on; and you will find she is the
Goddess—not of everybody's getting on—but only of
somebody's getting on. This is a vital, or rather

deathful, distinction. Examine it in your own ideal of the state of national life which this Goddess is to evoke and maintain. I asked you what it was, when I was last here;[1]—you have never told me. Now, shall I try to tell you?

Your ideal of human life then is, I think, that it should be passed in a pleasant undulating world, with iron and coal everywhere underneath it. On each pleasant bank of this world is to be a beautiful mansion, with two wings; and stables, and coachhouses; a moderately sized park; a large garden and hot-houses; and pleasant carriage drives through the shrubberies. In this mansion are to live the favoured votaries of the Goddess; the English gentleman, with his gracious wife, and his beautiful family; always able to have the boudoir and the jewels for the wife, and the beautiful ball dresses for the daughters, and hunters for the sons, and a shooting in the Highlands for himself. At the bottom of the bank, is to be the mill; not less than a quarter of a mile long, with a steam engine at each end, and two in the middle, and a chimney three hundred feet high. In this mill are to be in constant employment from eight hundred to a thousand workers, who never drink, never strike, always go to church on Sunday, and always express themselves in respectful language.

Is not that, broadly, and in the main features, the kind of thing you propose to yourselves? It is very pretty indeed, seen from above; not at all so pretty, seen from below. For, observe, while to one family this deity is indeed the Goddess of Getting-on, to a thousand families she is the Goddess of *not* Getting-on. " Nay," you say, " they have all their chance." Yes, so has every one in a lottery, but there must always be the same number of blanks. " Ah! but in a lottery it is not skill and intelligence which take the lead, but blind chance." What then! do you think the old practice, that " they should take who have the power,

[1] *Two Paths.*

and they should keep who can," is less iniquitous, when the power has become power of brains instead of fist? and that, though we may not take advantage of a child's or a woman's weakness, we may of a man's foolishness? "Nay, but finally, work must be done, and some one must be at the top, some one at the bottom." Granted, my friends. Work must always be, and captains of work must always be; and if you in the least remember the tone of any of my writings, you must know that they are thought unfit for this age, because they are always insisting on need of government, and speaking with scorn of liberty. But I beg you to observe that there is a wide difference between being captains or governors of work, and taking the profits of it. It does not follow, because you are general of an army, that you are to take all the treasure, or land, it wins (if it fight for treasure or land); neither, because you are king of a nation, that you are to consume all the profits of the nation's work. Real kings, on the contrary, are known invariably by their doing quite the reverse of this,—by their taking the least possible quantity of the nation's work for themselves. There is no test of real kinghood so infallible as that. Does the crowned creature live simply, bravely, un-ostentatiously? probably he *is* a King. Does he cover his body with jewels, and his table with delicates? in all probability he is *not* a King. It is possible he may be, as Solomon was; but that is when the nation shares his splendour with him. Solomon made gold, not only to be in his own palace as stones, but to be in Jerusalem as stones. But, even so, for the most part, these splendid kinghoods expire in ruin, and only the true kinghoods live, which are of royal labourers governing loyal labourers; who, both leading rough lives, establish the true dynasties. Conclusively you will find that because you are king of a nation, it does not follow that you are to gather for yourself all the wealth of that nation; neither, because you are king of a small part

of the nation, and lord over the means of its maintenance—over field, or mill, or mine, are you to take all
the produce of that piece of the foundation of national
existence for yourself.

You will tell me I need not preach against these
things, for I cannot mend them. No, good friends, I
cannot; but you can, and you will; or something else
can and will. Do you think these phenomena are to
stay always in their present power or aspect? All
history shows, on the contrary, that to be the exact
thing they never can do. Change *must* come; but it is
ours to determine whether change of growth, or change
of death. Shall the Parthenon be in ruins on its rock,
and Bolton priory in its meadow, but these mills of
yours be the consummation of the buildings of the
earth, and their wheels be as the wheels of eternity?
Think you that " men may come, and men may go,"
but—mills—go on for ever? Not so; out of these,
better or worse shall come; and it is for you to choose
which.

I know that none of this wrong is done with deliberate
purpose. I know, on the contrary, that you wish your
workmen well; that you do much for them, and that
you desire to do more for them, if you saw your way
to it, safely. I know that many of you have done,
and are every day doing, whatever you feel to be in
your power; and that even all this wrong and misery
are brought about by a warped sense of duty, each of
you striving to do his best, without noticing that this
best is essentially and centrally the best for himself,
not for others. And all this has come of the spreading
of that thrice accursed, thrice impious doctrine of the
modern economist, that, " To do the best for yourself,
is finally to do the best for others." Friends, our great
Master said not so; and most absolutely we shall find
this world is not made so. Indeed, to do the best for
others, is finally to do the best for ourselves; but it will
not do to have our eyes fixed on that issue. The Pagans

had got beyond that. Hear what a Pagan says of this matter; hear what were, perhaps, the last written words of Plato,—if not the last actually written, (for this we cannot know,) yet assuredly in fact and power his parting words—in which, endeavouring to give full crowning and harmonious close to all his thoughts, and to speak the sum of them by the imagined sentence of the Great Spirit, his strength and his heart fail him, and the words cease, broken off for ever. It is the close of the dialogue called "Critias," in which he describes, partly from real tradition, partly in ideal dream, the early state of Athens; and the genesis, and order, and religion, of the fabled isle of Atlantis; in which genesis he conceives the same first perfection and final degeneracy of man, which in our own Scriptural tradition is expressed by saying that the Sons of God intermarried with the daughters of men, for he supposes the earliest race to have been indeed the children of God; and to have corrupted themselves, until " their spot was not the spot of his children." And this, he says, was the end; that indeed " through many generations, so long as the God's nature in them yet was full, they were submissive to the sacred laws, and carried themselves lovingly to all that had kindred with them in divineness; for their uttermost spirit was faithful and true, and in every wise great; so that, in all meekness of wisdom, they dealt with each other, and took all the chances of life; and despising all things except virtue, they cared little what happened day by day, and *bore lightly the burden* of gold and of possessions; for they saw that, if only their common love and virtue increased, all these things would be increased together with them; but to set their esteem and ardent pursuit upon material possession, would be to lose that first, and their virtue and affection together with it. And by such reasoning, and what of the divine nature remained in them, they gained all this greatness of which we have already told; but when the God's part of them faded and became extinct, being mixed again and again, and effaced by the prevalent mortality; and the human nature at last exceeded, they then became unable to endure the courses of fortune; and fell into shapelessness of life, and baseness in the sight of him who could see, having lost everything that was fairest of their honour; while to the blind hearts which could not discern the true life, tending to happiness, it seemed that they were then chiefly noble and happy, being filled with all iniquity of inordinate possession and power. Whereupon, the God of Gods, whose King-hood is in laws, beholding a once just nation thus cast into misery, and desiring to lay such punishment upon them as might make them repent into restraining, gathered together all the gods into his dwelling place, which from heaven's centre overlooks whatever has part in creation; and having assembled them, he said "——

The rest is silence. So ended are the last words of the chief wisdom of the heathen, spoken of this idol of riches; this idol of yours; this golden image, high by measureless cubits, set up where your green fields of England are furnace-burnt into the likeness of the plain of Dura: this idol, forbidden to us, first of all idols, by our own Master and faith; forbidden to us also by every human lip that has ever, in any age or people, been accounted of as able to speak according to the purposes of God. Continue to make that for-bidden deity your principal one, and soon no more art, no more science, no more pleasure will be possible. Catastrophe will come; or, worse than catastrophe, slow mouldering and withering into Hades. But if you can fix some conception of a true human state of life to be striven for—life for all men as for your-selves—if you can determine some honest and simple order of existence; following those trodden ways of wisdom, which are pleasantness, and seeking her quiet and withdrawn paths, which are peace;—then, and so

sanctifying wealth into "commonwealth," all your
art, your literature, your daily labours, your domestic
affection, and citizen's duty, will join and increase into
one magnificent harmony. You will know then how to
build, well enough; you will build with stone well,
but with flesh better; temples not made with hands,
but riveted of hearts; and that kind of marble, crimson-
veined, is indeed eternal.

LECTURE III

WAR

LECTURE III

WAR

(*Delivered at the Royal Military Academy, Woolwich.*)

YOUNG SOLDIERS, I do not doubt but that many of you came unwillingly to-night, and many in merely contemptuous curiosity, to hear what a writer on painting could possibly say, or would venture to say, respecting your great art of war. You may well think within yourselves, that a painter might, perhaps without immodesty, lecture younger painters upon painting, but not young lawyers upon law, nor young physicians upon medicine—least of all, it may seem to you, young warriors upon war. And, indeed, when I was asked to address you, I declined at first, and declined long; for I felt that you would not be interested in my special business, and would certainly think there was small need for me to come to teach you yours. Nay, I knew that there ought to be *no* such need, for the great veteran soldiers of England are now men every way so thoughtful, so noble, and so good, that no other teaching than their knightly example, and their few words of grave and tried counsel, should be either necessary for you, or even, without assurance of due modesty in the offerer, endured by you.

But being asked, not once nor twice, I have not ventured persistently to refuse; and I will try, in very few words, to lay before you some reason why you should accept my excuse, and hear me patiently. You may imagine that your work is wholly foreign to, and separate from mine. So far from that, all the pure and

79

noble arts of peace are founded on war; no great art
ever yet rose on earth, but among a nation of soldiers.
There is no art among a shepherd people, if it remains
at peace.   There is no art among an agricultural people,
f it remains at peace.   Commerce is barely consistent
with fine art; but cannot produce it.   Manufacture not
only is unable to produce it, but invariably destroys
whatever seeds of it exist.   There is no great art possible
to a nation but that which is based on battle.

Now, though I hope you love fighting for its own sake,
you must, I imagine, be surprised at my assertion that
there is any such good fruit of fighting.   You supposed,
probably, that your office was to defend the works
of peace, but certainly not to found them: nay, the
common course of war, you may have thought, was only
to destroy them.   And truly, I, who tell you this of the
use of war, should have been the last of men to tell you
so, had I trusted my own experience only.   Hear why:
I have given a considerable part of my life to the investigation of Venetian painting; and the result of that
enquiry was my fixing upon one man as the greatest of
all Venetians, and therefore, as I believed, of all painters
whatsoever.   I formed this faith, (whether right or
wrong matters at present nothing,) in the supremacy
of the painter Tintoret, under a roof covered with his
pictures; and of those pictures, three of the noblest were
then in the form of shreds of ragged canvas, mixed up
with the laths of the roof, rent through by three Austrian
shells.   Now, it is not every lecturer who *could* tell you
that he had seen three of his favourite pictures torn to
rags by bomb-shells.   And after such a sight, it is not
every lecturer who *would* tell you that, nevertheless, war
was the foundation of all great art.

Yet the conclusion is inevitable, from any careful comparison of the states of great historic races at different
periods.   Merely to show you what I mean, I will sketch
for you, very briefly, the broad steps of the advance of
the best art of the world.   The first dawn of it is in

Egypt; and the power of it is founded on the perpetual contemplation of death, and of future judgment, by the mind of a nation of which the ruling caste were priests, and the second, soldiers. The greatest works produced by them are sculptures of their kings going out to battle, or receiving the homage of conquered armies. And you must remember also, as one of the great keys to the splendour of the Egyptian nation, that the priests were not occupied in theology only. Their theology was the basis of practical government and law; so that they were not so much priests as religious judges; the office of Samuel, among the Jews, being as nearly as possible correspondent to theirs.

All the rudiments of art then, and much more than the rudiments of all science, are laid first by this great warrior-nation, which held in contempt all mechanical trades, and in absolute hatred the peaceful life of shepherds. From Egypt art passes directly into Greece, where all poetry, and all painting, are nothing else than the description, praise, or dramatic representation of war, or of the exercises which prepare for it, in their connection with offices of religion. All Greek institutions had first respect to war; and their conception of it, as one necessary office of all human and divine life, is expressed simply by the images of their guiding gods. Apollo is the god of all wisdom of the intellect; he bears the arrow and the bow, before he bears the lyre. Again, Athena is the goddess of all wisdom in conduct. Yet it is by the helmet and the shield, oftener than by the shuttle, that she is distinguished from other deities.

There were, however, two great differences in principles between the Greek and the Egyptian theories of policy. In Greece there was no soldier caste; every citizen was necessarily a soldier. And, again, while the Greeks rightly despised mechanical arts as much as the Egyptians, they did not make the fatal mistake of despising agricultural and pastoral life; but perfectly honoured both. These two conditions of truer thought

F

raise them quite into the highest rank of wise manhood that has yet been reached; for all our great arts, and nearly all our great thoughts, have been borrowed or derived from them. Take away from us what they have given; and I hardly can imagine how low the modern European would stand.

Now, you are to remember, in passing to the next phase of history, that though you *must* have war to produce art—you must also have much more than war; namely, an art-instinct or genius in the people; and that, though all the talent for painting in the world won't make painters of you, unless you have a gift for fighting as well, you may have the gift for fighting, and none for painting. Now, in the next great dynasty of soldiers, the art-instinct is wholly wanting. I have not yet investigated the Roman character enough to tell you the causes of this; but I believe, paradoxical as it may seem to you, that, however truly the Roman might say of himself that he was born of Mars, and suckled by the wolf, he was nevertheless, at heart, more of a farmer than a soldier. The exercises of war were with him practical, not poetical; his poetry was in domestic life only, and the object of battle, *pacis imponere morem.* And the arts are extinguished in his hands, and do not rise again, until, with Gothic chivalry, there comes back into the mind of Europe a passionate delight in war itself, for the sake of war. And then, with the romantic knighthood which can imagine no other noble employment,—under the fighting kings of France, England, and Spain; and under the fighting dukeships and citizenships of Italy, art is born again, and rises to her height in the great valleys of Lombardy and Tuscany, through which there flows not a single stream, from all their Alps or Apennines, that did not once run dark red from battle: and it reaches its culminating glory in the city which gave to history the most intense type of soldiership yet seen among men;—the city whose armies were led in their assault by their king, led through it to victory by their king, and so led, though that king of theirs was blind, and in the extremity of his age.

And from this time forward, as peace is established or extended in Europe, the arts decline. They reach an unparalleled pitch of costliness, but lose their life, enlist themselves at last on the side of luxury and various corruption, and, among wholly tranquil nations, wither utterly away; remaining only in partial practice among races who, like the French and us, have still the minds, though we cannot all live the lives, of soldiers.

" It may be so," I can suppose that a philanthropist might exclaim. " Perish then the arts, if they can flourish only at such a cost. What worth is there in toys of canvas and stone, if compared to the joy and peace of artless domestic life? " And the answer is—truly, in themselves, none. But as expressions of the highest state of the human spirit, their worth is infinite. As results they may be worthless, but, as signs, they are above price. For it is an assured truth that, whenever the faculties of men are at their fullness, they *must* express themselves by art; and to say that a state is without such expression, is to say that it is sunk from its proper level of manly nature. So that, when I tell you that war is the foundation of all the arts, I mean also that it is the foundation of all the high virtues and faculties of men.

It was very strange to me to discover this; and very dreadful—but I saw it to be quite an undeniable fact. The common notion that peace and the virtues of civil life flourished together, I found to be wholly untenable. Peace and the *vices* of civil life only flourish together. We talk of peace and learning, and of peace and plenty, and of peace and civilisation; but I found that those were not the words which the Muse of History coupled together: that, on her lips, the words were—peace and sensuality, peace and selfishness, peace and corruption, peace and death. I found, in brief, that all great nations learned their truth of word, and strength of thought, in war; that they were nourished in war, and wasted by peace; taught by war, and deceived by peace; trained by war, and betrayed by peace;—in a word, that they were born in war, and expired in peace.

Yet now note carefully, in the second place, it is not *all* war of which this can be said—nor all dragon's teeth, which, sown, will start up into men. It is not the ravage of a barbarian wolf-flock, as under Genseric or Suwarrow; nor the habitual restlessness and rapine of mountaineers, as on the old borders of Scotland; nor the occasional struggle of a strong peaceful nation for its life, as in the wars of the Swiss with Austria; nor the contest of merely ambitious nations for extent of power, as in the wars of France under Napoleon, or the just terminated war in America. None of these forms of war build anything but tombs. But the creative or foundational war is that in which the natural restlessness and love of contest among men are disciplined, by consent, into modes of beautiful—though it may be fatal—play: in which the natural ambition and love of power of men are disciplined into the aggressive conquest of surrounding evil: and in which the natural instincts of self-defence are sanctified by the nobleness of the institutions, and purity of the households, which they are appointed to defend. To such war as this all men are born; in such war as this any man may happily die; and forth from such war as this have arisen, throughout the extent of past ages, all the highest sanctities and virtues of humanity.

I shall therefore divide the war of which I would speak to you into three heads. War for exercise or play; war for dominion; and, war for defence.

I. And first, of war for exercise or play. I speak of it primarily in this light, because, through all past history, manly war has been more an exercise than anything else, among the classes who cause, and proclaim it. It is not a game to the conscript, or the pressed sailor; but neither of these are the causers of it. To

the governor who determines that war shall be, and to
the youths who voluntarily adopt it as their profession,
it has always been a grand pastime; and chiefly pursued because they had nothing else to do. And this
is true without any exception. No king whose mind
was fully occupied with the development of the inner
resources of his kingdom, or with any other sufficing subject of thought, ever entered into war but on compulsion.
No youth who was earnestly busy with any peaceful
subject of study, or set on any serviceable course of
action, ever voluntarily became a soldier. Occupy him,
early and wisely, in agriculture or business, in science or
in literature, and he will never think of war otherwise
than as a calamity. But leave him idle; and, the more
brave and active and capable he is by nature, the more
he will thirst for some appointed field for action; and
find, in the passion and peril of battle, the only satisfy-
ing fulfilment of his unoccupied being. And from the
earliest incipient civilisation until now, the population
of the earth divides itself, when you look at it widely,
into two races; one of workers, and the other of players
—one tilling the ground, manufacturing, building, and
otherwise providing for the necessities of life;—the other
part proudly idle, and continually therefore needing
recreation, in which they use the productive and laborious orders partly as their cattle, and partly as their
puppets or pieces in the game of death.

Now, remember, whatever virtue or goodliness there
may be in this game of war, rightly played, there is none
when you thus play it with a multitude of small human
pawns.

If you, the gentlemen of this or any other kingdom,
choose to make your pastime of contest, do so, and
welcome; but set not up these unhappy peasant-pieces
upon the green fielded board. If the wager is to be of
death, lay it on your own heads, not theirs. A goodly
struggle in the Olympic dust, though it be the dust of
the grave, the gods will look upon, and be with you in;

but they will not be with you, if you sit on the sides of
the amphitheatre, whose steps are the mountains of
earth, whose arena its valleys, to urge your peasant
millions into gladiatorial war.   You also, you tender
and delicate women, for whom, and by whose command,
all true battle has been, and must ever be; you would
perhaps shrink now, though you need not, from the
thought of sitting as queens above set lists where the
jousting game might be mortal.   How much more, then,
ought you to shrink from the thought of sitting above a
theatre pit in which even a few condemned slaves were
slaying each other only for your delight!   And do you
not shrink from the *fact* of sitting above a theatre pit,
where,—not condemned slaves,—but the best and
bravest of the poor sons of your people, slay each other,
—not man to man,—as the coupled gladiators; but
race to race, in duel of generations?   You would tell me,
perhaps, that you do not sit to see this; and it is indeed
true, that the women of Europe—those who have no
heart-interest of their own at peril in the contest—draw
the curtains of their boxes, and muffle the openings;
so that from the pit of the circus of slaughter there may
reach them only at intervals a half-heard cry and a
murmur as of the wind's sighing, when myriads of souls
expire.   They shut out the death-cries; and are happy,
and talk wittily among themselves.   That is the utter
literal fact of what our ladies do in their pleasant lives.

Nay, you might answer, speaking for them—" We do
not let these wars come to pass for our play, nor by our
carelessness; we cannot help them.   How can any final
quarrel of nations be settled otherwise than by war? "
I cannot now delay, to tell you how political quarrels
might be otherwise settled.   But grant that they cannot.
Grant that no law of reason can be understood by
nations; no law of justice submitted to by them: and
that, while questions of a few acres, and of petty cash,
can be determined by truth and equity, the questions
which are to issue in the perishing or saving of kingdoms

can be determined only by the truth of the sword, and
the equity of the rifle. Grant this, and even then, judge
if it will always be necessary for you to put your quarrel
into the hearts of your poor, and sign your treaties with
peasants' blood. You would be ashamed to do this in
your own private position and power. Why should you
not be ashamed also to do it in public place and power?
If you quarrel with your neighbour, and the quarrel be
indeterminable by law, and mortal, you and he do not
send your footmen to Battersea fields to fight it out;
nor do you set fire to his tenants' cottages, nor spoil
their goods. You fight out your quarrel yourselves, and
at your own danger, if at all. And you do not think
it materially affects the arbitrement that one of you has
a larger household than the other; so that, if the
servants or tenants were brought into the field with
their masters, the issue of the contest could not be
doubtful? You either refuse the private duel, or you
practise it under laws of honour, not of physical force;
that so it may be, in a manner, justly concluded. Now
the just or unjust conclusion of the private feud is of
little moment, while the just or unjust conclusion of the
public feud is of eternal moment: and yet, in this public
quarrel, you take your servants' sons from their arms to
fight for it, and your servants' food from their lips to
support it; and the black seals on the parchment of your
treaties of peace are the deserted hearth and the fruitless field. There is a ghastly ludicrousness in this, as
there is mostly in these wide and universal crimes. Hear
the statement of the very fact of it in the most literal
words of the greatest of our English thinkers:—

" What, speaking in quite unofficial language, is the
net-purport and upshot of war? To my own knowledge,
for example, there dwell and toil, in the British village of
Dumdrudge, usually some five-hundred souls. From
these, by certain ' natural enemies ' of the French there
are successively selected, during the French war, say

thirty able-bodied men. Dumdrudge, at her own
expense, has suckled and nursed them; she has, not
without difficulty and sorrow, fed them up to manhood,
and even trained them to crafts, so that one can weave,
another build, another hammer, and the weakest can
stand under thirty stone avoirdupois.   Nevertheless,
amid much weeping and swearing, they are selected;
all dressed in red; and shipped away, at the public
charges, some two thousand miles, or say only to the
south of Spain; and fed there till wanted.

" And now to that same spot in the south of Spain are
thirty similar French artisans, from a French Dumdrudge, in like manner wending; till at length, after
infinite effort, the two parties come into actual juxta-
position; and Thirty stands fronting Thirty, each with
a gun in his hand.

" Straightway the word ' Fire!' is given, and they
blow the souls out of one another, and in place of sixty
brisk useful craftsmen, the world has sixty dead car-
cases, which it must bury, and anon shed tears for.
Had these men any quarrel?   Busy as the devil is, not
the smallest!   They lived far enough apart; were the
entirest strangers; nay, in so wide a universe, there was
even, unconsciously, by commerce, some mutual help-
fulness between them.   How then?   Simpleton!   their
governors had fallen out; and instead of shooting one
another, had the cunning to make these poor block-
heads shoot." (*Sartor Resartus.*)

Positively, then, gentlemen, the game of battle must
not, and shall not, ultimately be played this way.   But
should it be played any way?   Should it, if not by your
servants, be practised by yourselves?   I think, yes.
Both history and human instinct seem alike to say,
yes.   All healthy men like fighting, and like the sense
of danger; all brave women like to hear of their fighting, and of their facing danger.   This is a fixed instinct
in the fine race of them; and I cannot help fancying

that fair fight in the best play for them; and that a tournament was a better game than a steeplechase. The time may perhaps come in France as well as here, for universal hurdle-races and cricketing: but I do not think universal " crickets " will bring out the best qualities of the nobles of either country. I use, in such question, the test which I have adopted, of the connection of war with other arts; and I reflect how, as a sculptor, I should feel, if I were asked to design a monument for a dead knight, in Westminster Abbey, with a carving of a bat at one end, and a ball at the other. It may be the remains in me only of savage Gothic prejudice; but I had rather carve it with a shield at one end, and a sword at the other. And this, observe, with no reference whatever to any story of duty done, or cause defended. Assume the knight merely to have ridden out occasionally to fight his neighbour for exercise; assume him even a soldier of fortune, and to have gained his bread, and filled his purse, at the sword's point. Still, I feel as if it were, somehow, grander and worthier in him to have made his bread by sword play than any other play; I had rather he had made it by thrusting than by batting;—much more, than by betting. Much rather that he should ride war horses, than back race horses; and—I say it sternly and deliberately—much rather would I have him slay his neighbour, than cheat him.

But remember, so far as this may be true, the game of war is only that in which the *full personal power of the human creature* is brought out in management of its weapons. And this for three reasons:—

First, the great justification of this game is that it truly, when well played, determines *who is the best man ;* —who is the highest bred, the most self-denying, the most fearless, the coolest of nerve, the swiftest of eye and hand. You cannot test these qualities wholly, unless there is a clear possibility of the struggle's ending in death. It is only in the fronting of that condition that the full trial of the man, soul and body, comes out. You may go to your game of wickets, or of hurdles, or of cards, and any knavery that is in you may stay unchallenged all the while. But if the play may be ended at any moment by a lance-thrust, a man will probably make up his accounts a little before he enters it. Whatever is rotten and evil in him will weaken his hand more in holding a sword hilt, than in balancing a billiard cue; and on the whole, the habit of living lightly hearted, in daily presence of death, always has had, and must have, a tendency both to the making and testing of honest men. But for the final testing, observe, you must make the issue of battle strictly dependent on fineness of frame, and firmness of hand. You must not make it the question, which of the combatants has the longest gun, or which has got behind the biggest tree, or which has the wind in his face, or which has gunpowder made by the best chemists, or iron smelted with the best coal, or the angriest mob at his back. Decide your battle, whether of nations or individuals, on *those* terms;—and you have only multiplied confusion, and added slaughter to iniquity. But decide your battle by pure trial which has the strongest arm, and steadiest heart,—and you have gone far to decide a great many matters besides, and to decide them rightly.

And the other reasons for this mode of decision of cause, are the diminution both of the material destructiveness, or cost, and of the physical distress of war. For you must not think that in speaking to you in this, (as you may imagine,) fantastic praise of battle, I have overlooked the conditions weighing against me. I pray all of you, who have not read, to read with the most earnest attention, Mr. Helps' two essays, on War, and Government, in the first volume of the last series of *Friends in Council.* Everything that can be urged against war is there simply, exhaustively, and most graphically stated. And all, there urged, is true. But

the two great counts of evil alleged against war by that
most thoughtful writer, hold only against modern war.
If you have to take away masses of men from all industrial employment,—to feed them by the labour of
others,—to move them and provide them with destruc-
tive machines, varied daily in national rivalship of in-
ventive cost; if you have to ravage the country which
you attack,—to destroy, for a score of future years, its
roads, its woods, its cities, and its harbours;—and if,
finally, having brought masses of men, counted by
hundreds of thousands, face to face, you tear those
masses to pieces with jagged shot, and leave the frag-
ments of living creatures, countlessly beyond all help of
surgery, to starve and parch, through days of torture,
down into clots of clay—what book of account shall
record the cost of your work;—What book of judgment
sentence the guilt of it?

That, I say, is *modern* war,—scientific war,—chemical
and mechanic war,—worse even than the savage's
poisoned arrow. And yet you will tell me, perhaps,
that any other war than this is impossible now. It may
be so; the progress of science cannot, perhaps, be otherwise registered than by new facilities of destruction;
and the brotherly love of our enlarging Christianity be
only proved by multiplication of murder. Yet hear,
for a moment, what war was, in Pagan and ignorant
days;—what war might yet be, if we could extinguish
our science in darkness, and join the heathen's practice
to the Christian's theory. I read you this from a book
which probably most of you know well, and all ought to
know—Muller's *Dorians ;*—but I have put the points I
wish you to remember in closer connection than in his
text.

" The chief characteristic of the warriors of Sparta
was great composure and a subdued strength; the
violence (λύσσα) of Aristodemus and Isadas being considered as deserving rather of blame than praise; and

these qualities in general distinguished the Greeks from the northern Barbarians, whose boldness always consisted in noise and tumult. For the same reason the Spartans *sacrificed to the Muses* before an action; these goddesses being expected to produce regularity and order in battle; as they *sacrificed on the same occasion in Crete to the god of love*, as the confirmer of mutual esteem and shame. Every man put on a crown, when the band of flute-players gave the signal for attack; all the shields of the line glittered with their high polish, and mingled their splendour with the dark red of the purple mantles, which were meant both to adorn the combatant, and to conceal the blood of the wounded; to fall well and decorously being an incentive the more to the most heroic valour. The conduct of the Spartans in battle denotes a high and noble disposition, which rejected all the extremes of brutal rage. The pursuit of the enemy ceased when the victory was completed; and after the signal for retreat had been given, all hostilities ceased. The spoiling of arms, at least during the battle, was also interdicted; and the consecration of the spoils of slain enemies to the gods, as, in general, all rejoicings for victory, were considered as ill-omened."

Such was the war of the greatest soldiers who prayed to heathen gods. What Christian war is, preached by Christian ministers, let any one tell you, who saw the sacred crowning, and heard the sacred flute-playing, and was inspired and sanctified by the divinely-measured and musical language, of any North American regiment preparing for its charge. And what is the relative cost of life in pagan and Christian wars, let this one fact tell you:—the Spartans won the decisive battle of Corinth with the loss of eight men; the victors at indecisive Gettysburg confess to the loss of 30,000.

II. I pass now to our second order of war, the commonest among men, that undertaken in desire of dominion. And let me ask you to think for a few moments what the real meaning of this desire of dominion is—first in the minds of kings—then in that of nations.

Now, mind you this first,—that I speak either about kings, or masses of men, with a fixed conviction that human nature is a noble and beautiful thing; not a foul nor a base thing. All the sin of men I esteem as their disease, not their nature; as a folly which may be prevented, not a necessity which must be accepted. And my wonder, even when things are at their worst, is always at the height which this human nature can attain. Thinking it high, I find it always a higher thing than I thought it; while those who think it low, find it, and will find it, always, lower than they thought it: the fact being, that it is infinite, and capable of infinite height and infinite fall; but the nature of it— and here is the faith which I would have you hold with me—the *nature* of it is in the nobleness, not in the catastrophe.

Take the faith in its utmost terms. When the captain of the *London* shook hands with his mate, saying, "God speed you! I will go down with my passengers," *that* I believe to be "human nature." He does not do it from any religious motive,—from any hope of reward, or any fear of punishment; he does it because he is a man. But when a mother, living among the fair fields of merry England, gives her two-year-old child to be suffocated under a mattrass in her inner room, while the said mother waits and talks outside; *that* I believe to be *not* human nature. You have the two extremes there, shortly. And you, men, and mothers, who are here face to face with me to-night, I call upon you to say which of these is human, and which inhuman,—which "natural" and which "unnatural"? Choose your creed at once, I beseech you:—choose it with unshaken choice,—choose it for ever. Will you take, for foundation of act and hope, the faith that this man was such as God made him, or that this woman was such as God made her? Which of them has failed

from their nature,—from their present, possible, actual
nature;—not their nature of long ago, but their nature
of now? Which has betrayed it—falsified it? Did
the guardian who died in his trust, die inhumanly, and
as a fool; and did the murderess of her child fulfil the
law of her being? Choose, I say; infinitude of choices
hang upon this. You have had false prophets among
you,—for centuries you have had them,—solemnly
warned against them though you were; false prophets,
who have told you that all men are nothing but fiends
or wolves, half beast, half devil. Believe that, and
indeed you may sink to that. But refuse that, and
have faith that God " made you upright," though *you*
have sought out many inventions; so, you will strive
daily to become more what your Maker meant and
means you to be, and daily gives you also the power
to be,—and you will cling more and more to the nobleness and virtue that is in you, saying, " My righteousness I hold fast, and will not let it go."

I have put this to you as a choice, as if you might
hold either of these creeds you liked best. But there
is in reality no choice for you; the facts being quite
easily ascertainable. You have no business to *think*
about this matter, or to choose in it. The broad fact
is, that a human creature of the highest race, and most
perfect as a human thing, is invariably both kind and
true; and that as you lower the race, you get cruelty
and falseness, as you get deformity: and this so steadily
and assuredly, that the two great words which, in their
first use, meant only perfection of race, have come,
by consequence of the invariable connection of virtue
with the fine human nature, both to signify benevolence
of disposition. The word generous, and the word
gentle, both, in their origin, meant only " of pure race,"
but because charity and tenderness are inseparable
from this purity of blood, the words which once stood
only for pride, now stand as synonyms for virtue.

Now, this being the true power of our inherent

The Crown of Wild Olive

humanity, and seeing that all the aim of education
should be to develop this;—and seeing also what
magnificent self-sacrifice the higher classes of men are
capable of, for any cause that they understand or feel,—
it is wholly inconceivable to me how well-educated
princes, who ought to be of all gentlemen the gentlest,
and of all nobles the most generous, and whose title of
royalty means only their function of doing every man
" *right* "—how these, I say, throughout history, should
so rarely pronounce themselves on the side of the poor
and of justice, but continually maintain themselves and
their own interests by oppression of the poor, and by
wresting of justice; and how this should be accepted
as so natural, that the word loyalty, which means faith-
fulness to law, is used as if it were only the duty of a
people to be loyal to their king, and not the duty of a
king to be infinitely more loyal to his people. How
comes it to pass that a captain will die with his passengers, and lean over the gunwale to give the parting
boat its course; but that a king will not usually die
with, much less *for*, his passengers—thinks it rather
incumbent on his passengers, in any number, to die
for *him?* Think, I beseech you, of the wonder of this.
The sea captain, not captain by divine right, but only
by company's appointment;—not a man of royal
descent, but only a plebeian who can steer;—not with
the eyes of the world upon him, but with feeble chance,
depending on one poor boat, of his name being ever
heard above the wash of the fatal waves;—not with
the cause of a nation resting on his act, but helpless to
save so much as a child from among the lost crowd with
whom he resolves to be lost,—yet goes down quietly
to his grave, rather than break his faith to these few
emigrants. But your captain by divine right,—your
captain with the hues of a hundred shields of kings upon
his breast,—your captain whose every deed, brave or
base, will be illuminated or branded for ever before
unescapable eyes of men,—your captain whose every

thought and act are beneficent, or fatal, from sun-rising to setting, blessing as the sunshine, or shadowing as the night,—this captain, as you find him in history, for the most part thinks only how he may tax his passengers, and sit at most ease in his state cabin!

For observe, if there had been indeed in the hearts of the rulers of great multitudes of men any such con-ception of work for the good of those under their com-mand, as there is in the good and thoughtful masters of any small company of men, not only wars for the sake of mere increase of power could never take place, but our idea of power itself would be entirely altered. Do you suppose that to think and act even for a million of men, to hear their complaints, watch their weaknesses, restrain their vices, make laws for them, lead them, day by day, to purer life, is not enough for one man's work? If any of us were absolute lord only of a district of a hundred miles square, and were resolved on doing our utmost for it; making it feed as large a number of people as possible; making every clod productive, and every rock defensive, and every human being happy; should we not have enough on our hands think you? But if the ruler has any other aim than this; if, careless of the result of his interference, he desire only the authority to interfere; and, regardless of what is ill-done or well-done, cares only that it shall be done at his bidding;—if he would rather do two hundred miles' space of mischief, than one hundred miles' space of good, of course he will try to add to his territory; and to add illimitably. But does he add to his power? Do you call it power in a child, if he is allowed to play with the wheels and bands of some vast engine, pleased with their murmur and whirl, till his unwise touch, wander-ing where it ought not, scatters beam and wheel into ruin? Yet what machine is so vast, so incognisable, as the working of the mind of a nation; what child's touch so wanton, as the word of a selfish king? And yet, how long have we allowed the historian to speak

of the extent of the calamity a man causes, as a just
ground for his pride; and to extol him as the greatest
prince, who is only the centre of the widest error.
Follow out this thought by yourselves; and you will
find that all power, properly so called, is wise and
benevolent.   There may be capacity in a drifting fire-
ship to destroy a fleet; there may be venom enough
in a dead body to infect a nation:—but which of you,
the most ambitious, would desire a drifting kinghood,
robed in consuming fire, or a poison-dipped sceptre
whose touch was mortal?   There is no true potency,
remember, but that of help; nor true ambition, but
ambition to save.

And then, observe farther, this true power, the power
of saving, depends neither on multitude of men, nor on
extent of territory.   We are continually assuming that
nations become strong according to their numbers.
They indeed become so, if those numbers can be made
of one mind; but how are you sure you can stay them
in one mind, and keep them from having north and
south minds?   Grant them unanimous, how know you
they will be unanimous in right?   If they are unanimous in wrong, the more they are, essentially the
weaker they are.   Or, suppose that they can neither
be of one mind, nor of two minds, but can only be of
no mind?   Suppose they are a mere helpless mob;
tottering into precipitant catastrophe, like a waggon
load of stones when the wheel comes off.   Dangerous
enough for their neighbours, certainly, but not
" powerful."

Neither does strength depend on extent of territory,
any more than upon number of population.   Take
up your maps when you go home this evening,—put
the cluster of British Isles beside the mass of South
America; and then consider whether any race of men
need care how much ground they stand upon.   The
strength is in the men, and in their unity and virtue,
not in their standing room: a little group of wise hearts

G

is better than a wilderness full of fools; and only that
nation gains true territory, which gains itself.

And now for the brief practical outcome of all this.
Remember, no government is ultimately strong, but
in proportion to its kindness and justice; and that a
nation does not strengthen, by merely multiplying and
diffusing itself. We have not strengthened as yet, by
multiplying into America. Nay, even when it has not
to encounter the separating conditions of emigration,
a nation need not boast itself of multiplying on its own
ground, if it multiplies only as flies or locusts do, with
the god of flies for its god. It multiplies its strength
only by increasing as one great family, in perfect
fellowship and brotherhood. And lastly, it does not
strengthen itself by seizing dominion over races whom
it cannot benefit. Austria is not strengthened, but
weakened, by her grasp of Lombardy; and whatever
apparent increase of majesty and of wealth may have
accrued to us from the possession of India, whether
these prove to us ultimately power or weakness, depends
wholly on the degree in which our influence on the
native race shall be benevolent and exalting. But,
as it is at their own peril that any race extends their
dominion in mere desire of power, so it is at their own
still greater peril that they refuse to undertake aggressive war, according to their force, whenever they are
assured that their authority would be helpful and protective. Nor need you listen to any sophistical objection of the impossibility of knowing when a people's
help is needed, or when not. Make your national
conscience clean, and your national eyes will soon be
clear. No man who is truly ready to take part in a
noble quarrel will ever stand long in doubt by whom,
or in what cause, his aid is needed. I hold it my duty
to make no political statement of any special bearing
in this presence; but I tell you broadly and boldly,
that, within these last ten years, we English have,
as a knightly nation, lost our spurs: we have fought

where we should not have fought, for gain; and we have been passive where we should not have been passive, for fear. I tell you that the principle of non-intervention, as now preached among us, is as selfish and cruel as the worst frenzy of conquest, and differs from it only by being, not only malignant, but dastardly.

I know, however, that my opinions on this subject differ too widely from those ordinarily held, to be any farther intruded upon you; and therefore I pass lastly to examine the conditions of the third kind of noble war;—war waged simply for defence of the country in which we were born, and for the maintenance and execution of her laws, by whomsoever threatened or defied. It is to this duty that I suppose most men entering the army consider themselves in reality to be bound, and I want you now to reflect what the laws of mere defence are; and what the soldier's duty, as now understood, or supposed to be understood. You have solemnly devoted yourselves to be English soldiers, for the guardianship of England. I want you to feel what this vow of yours indeed means, or is gradually coming to mean. You take it upon you, first, while you are sentimental schoolboys; you go into your military convent, or barracks, just as a girl goes into her convent while she is a sentimental schoolgirl; neither of you then know what you are about, though both the good soldiers and good nuns make the best of it afterwards. You don't understand perhaps why I call you " senti-mental " schoolboys, when you go into the army? Because, on the whole, it is the love of adventure, of excitement, of fine dress and of the pride of fame, all which are sentimental motives, which chiefly make a boy like going into the Guards better than into a count-ing-house. You fancy, perhaps, that there is a severe sense of duty mixed with these peacocky motives? And in the best of you, there is; but do not think that it is principal. If you cared to do your duty to your country in a prosaic and unsentimental way, depend upon it, there is now truer duty to be done in raising harvests, than in burning them; more in building houses, than in shelling them—more in winning money by your own work, wherewith to help men, than in taxing other people's work, for money wherewith to slay men;—more duty finally, in honest and unselfish living than in honest and unselfish dying, though that seems to your boys' eyes the bravest.   So far then, as for your own honour, and the honour of your families, you choose brave death in a red coat before brave life in a black one, you are sentimental; and now see what this passionate vow of yours comes to.   For a little while you ride, and you hunt tigers or savages, you shoot, and are shot; you are happy, and proud, always, and honoured and wept if you die; and you are satisfied with your life, and with the end of it; believing, on the whole, that good rather than harm of it comes to others, and much pleasure to you.   But as the sense of duty enters into your forming minds, the vow takes another aspect.   You find that you have put yourselves into the hand of your country as a weapon.   You have vowed to strike, when she bids you, and to stay scabbarded when she bids you; all that you need answer for is, that you fail not in her grasp.   And there is goodness in this, and greatness, if you can trust the hand and heart of the Britomart who has braced you to her side, and are assured that when she leaves you sheathed in darkness, there is no need for your flash to the sun. But remember, good and noble as this state may be, it is a state of slavery.   There are different kinds of slaves and different masters.   Some slaves are scourged to their work by whips, others are scourged to it by restlessness or ambition.   It does not matter what the whip is; it is none the less a whip, because you have cut thongs for it out of your own souls: the fact, so far, of slavery, is in being driven to your work without thought, at another's bidding.   Again, some slaves are bought with money, and others with praise.   It matters

not what the purchase-money is. The distinguishing
sign of slavery is to have a price, and be bought for it.
Again, it matters not what kind of work you are set on;
some slaves are set to forced diggings, others to forced
marches; some dig furrows, others field-works, and
others graves. Some press the juice of reeds, and some
the juice of vines, and some the blood of men. The
fact of the captivity is the same whatever work we are
set upon, though the fruits of the toil may be different.
But, remember, in thus vowing ourselves to be the
slaves of any master, it ought to be some subject of
forethought with us, what work he is likely to put
us upon. You may think that the whole duty of a
soldier is to be passive, that it is the country you have
left behind who is to command, and you have only to
obey. But are you sure that you have left *all* your
country behind, or that the part of it you have so left
is indeed the best part of it? Suppose—and, remember,
it is quite conceivable—that you yourselves are indeed
the best part of England; that you, who have become
the slaves, ought to have been the masters; and that
those who are the masters, ought to have been the
slaves! If it is a noble and whole-hearted England,
whose bidding you are bound to do, it is well; but if
you are yourselves the best of her heart, and the
England you have left be but a half-hearted England,
how say you of your obedience? You were too proud
to become shop-keepers: are you satisfied then to
become the servants of shop-keepers? You were too
proud to become merchants or farmers yourselves:
will you have merchants or farmers, then, for your
field-marshals? You had no gifts of special grace for
Exeter Hall: will you have some gifted person thereat
for your commander-in-chief, to judge of your work,
and reward it? You imagine yourselves to be the army
of England: how if you should find yourselves, at last,
only the police of her manufacturing towns, and the
beadles of her little Bethels?

It is not so yet, nor will be so, I trust, for ever; but what I want you to see, and to be assured of, is, that the ideal of soldiership is not mere passive obedience and bravery; that, so far from this, no country is in a healthy state which has separated, even in a small degree, her civil from her military power. All states of the world, however great, fall at once when they use mercenary armies; and although it is a less instant form of error, (because involving no national taint of cowardice,) it is yet an error no less ultimately fatal—it is the error especially of modern times, of which we cannot yet know all the calamitous consequences,—to take away the best blood and strength of the nation, all the soul-substance of it that is brave, and careless of reward, and scornful of pain, and faithful in trust; and to cast that into steel, and make a mere sword of it; taking away its voice and will; but to keep the worst part of the nation—whatever is cowardly, avaricious, sensual, and faithless—and to give to this the voice, to this the authority, to this the chief privilege, where there is least capacity, of thought. The fulfilment of your vow for the defence of England will by no means consist in carrying out such a system. You are not true soldiers, if you only mean to stand at a shop-door, to protect shop-boys who are cheating inside. A soldier's vow to his country is that he will die for the guardianship of her domestic virtue, of her righteous laws, and of her any-way challenged or endangered honour. A state without virtue, without laws, and without honour, he is bound *not* to defend; nay, bound to redress by his own right hand that which he sees to be base in her. So sternly is this the law of Nature and life, that a nation once utterly corrupt can only be redeemed by a military despotism—never by talking, nor by its free effort. And the health of any state consists simply in this; that in it, those who are wisest shall also be strongest; its rulers should be also its soldiers; or, rather, by force of intellect more than of sword, its soldiers also its rulers. Whatever the hold which the aristocracy of England has on the heart of England, in that they are still always in front of her battles, this hold will not be enough, unless they are also in front of her thoughts. And truly her thoughts need good captain's leading now, if ever! Do you know what, by this beautiful division of labour (her brave men fighting, and her cowards thinking), she has come at last to think? Here is a bit of a paper in my hand,[1] a good one too, and an honest one; quite representative of the best common public thought of England at this moment; and it is holding forth in one of its leaders upon our " social welfare,"—upon our " vivid life "—upon the " political supremacy of Great Britain." And what do you think all these are owing to? To what our English sires have done for us, and taught us, age after age? No: not to that. To our honesty of heart, or coolness of head, or steadiness of will? No: not to these. To our thinkers, or our statesmen, or our poets, or our captains, or our martyrs, or the patient labour of our poor? No: not to these; or at least not to these in any chief measure. Nay, says the journal, " more than any agency, it is the cheapness and abundance of our coal which have made us what we are." If it be so, then " ashes to ashes " be our epitaph! and the sooner the better. I tell you, Gentlemen of England, if ever you would have your country breathe the pure breath of heaven again, and receive again a soul

[1] I do not care to refer to the journal quoted, because the article was unworthy of its general tone, though in order to enable the audience to verify the quoted sentence, I left the number containing it on the table, when I gave this lecture. But a saying of Baron Liebig's, quoted at the head of a leader on the same subject in the *Daily Telegraph* of January 11, 1866, summarily digests and presents the maximum folly of modern thought in this respect. " Civilisation," says the Baron, " is the economy of power, and English power is coal." Not altogether so, my chemical friend. Civilisation is the making of civil persons, which is a kind of distillation of which alembics are incapable, and does not at all imply the turning of a small company of gentlemen into a large company of ironmongers. And English power, (what little of it may be left) is by no means coal, but, indeed, of that which, " when the whole world turns to coal, then chiefly lives."

into her body, instead of rotting into a carcase, blown up in the belly with carbonic acid (and great *that* way), you must think, and feel, for your England, as well as fight for her: you must teach her that all the true greatness she ever had, or ever can have, she won while her fields were green and her faces ruddy;—that greatness is still possible for Englishmen, even though the ground be not hollow under their feet, nor the sky black over their heads;—and that, when the day comes for their country to lay her honours in the dust, her crest will not rise from it more loftily because it is dust of coal. Gentlemen, I tell you, solemnly, that the day is coming when the soldiers of England must be her tutors; and the captains of her army, captains also of her mind.

And now, remember, you soldier youths, who are thus in all ways the hope of your country; or must be, if she have any hope: remember that your fitness for all future trust depends upon what you are now. No good soldier in his old age was ever careless or indolent in his youth. Many a giddy and thoughtless boy has become a good bishop, or a good lawyer, or a good merchant; but no such an one ever became a good general. I challenge you, in all history, to find a record of a good soldier who was not grave and earnest in his youth. And, in general, I have no patience with people who talk about " the thoughtlessness of youth " indulgently. I had infinitely rather hear of thoughtless old age, and the indulgence due to *that*. When a man has done his work, and nothing can any way be materially altered in his fate, let him forget his toil, and jest with his fate, if he will; but what excuse can you find for wilfulness of thought, at the very time when every crisis of future fortune hangs on your decisions? A youth thoughtless! when all the happiness of his home for ever depends on the chances, or the passions, of an hour! A youth thoughtless! when the career of all his days depends on the opportunity of a moment! A youth thoughtless! when his every act is a foundation-stone of future con-

The Crown of Wild Olive

duct, and every imagination a fountain of life or death!
Be thoughtless in *any* after years, rather than now—
though, indeed, there is only one place where a man
may be nobly thoughtless,—his deathbed. No thinking
should ever be left to be done there.

Having, then, resolved that you will not waste recklessly, but earnestly use, these early days of yours,
remember that all the duties of her children to England
may be summed in two words—industry, and honour.
I say first, industry, for it is in this that soldier youth
are especially tempted to fail. Yet, surely, there is no
reason, because your life may possibly or probably be
shorter than other men's, that you should therefore
waste more recklessly the portion of it that is granted
you; neither do the duties of your profession, which
require you to keep your bodies strong, in any wise
involve the keeping of your minds weak. So far from
that, the experience, the hardship, and the activity of
a soldier's life render his powers of thought more accurate than those of other men; and while, for others, all
knowledge is often little more than a means of amusement, there is no form of science which a soldier may
not at some time or other find bearing on business of life
and death. A young mathematician may be excused
for languor in studying curves to be described only with
a pencil; but not in tracing those which are to be described with a rocket. Your knowledge of a wholesome
herb may involve the feeding of an army; and acquaintance with an obscure point of geography, the success of
a campaign. Never waste an instant's time, therefore;
the sin of idleness is a thousand-fold greater in you than
in other youths; for the fates of those who will one day
be under your command hang upon your knowledge;
lost moments now will be lost lives then, and every
instant which you carelessly take for play, you buy with
blood. But there is one way of wasting time, of all the
vilest, because it wastes, not time only, but the interest
and energy of your minds. Of all the ungentlemanly

habits into which you can fall, the vilest is betting, or interesting yourselves in the issues of betting. It unites nearly every condition of folly and vice; you concentrate your interest upon a matter of chance, instead of upon a subject of true knowledge; and you back opinions which you have no grounds for forming, merely because they are your own. All the insolence of egotism is in this; and so far as the love of excitement is complicated with the hope of winning money, you turn yourselves into the basest sort of tradesmen—those who live by speculation. Were there no other ground for industry, this would be a sufficient one; that it protected you from the temptation to so scandalous a vice. Work faithfully, and you will put yourselves in possession of a glorious and enlarging happiness; not such as can be won by the speed of a horse, or marred by the obliquity of a ball.

First, then, by industry you must fulfil your vow to your country; but all industry and earnestness will be useless unless they are consecrated by your resolution to be in all things men of honour; not honour in the common sense only, but in the highest. Rest on the force of the two main words in the great verse, *integer* vitæ, scelerisque *purus*. You have vowed your life to England; give it her wholly—a bright, stainless, perfect life—a knightly life. Because you have to fight with machines instead of lances, there may be a necessity for more ghastly danger, but there is none for less worthiness of character, than in olden time. You may be true knights yet, though perhaps not *equites;* you may have to call yourselves " canonry " instead of " chivalry," but that is no reason why you should not call yourselves true men. So the first thing you have to see to in becoming soldiers is that you make yourselves wholly true. Courage is a mere matter of course among any ordinarily well-born youths; but neither truth nor gentleness is matter of course. You must bind them like shields about your necks; you must write

them on the tables of your hearts. Though it be not
exacted of you, yet exact it of yourselves, this vow of
stainless truth. Your hearts are, if you leave them un-
stirred, as tombs in which a god lies buried. Vow yourselves crusaders to redeem that sacred sepulchre. And
remember, before all things—for no other memory will
be so protective of you—that the highest law of this
knightly truth is that under which it is vowed to women.
Whomsoever else you deceive, whomsoever you injure,
whomsoever you leave unaided, you must not deceive,
nor injure, nor leave unaided, according to your power,
any woman of whatever rank. Believe me, every
virtue of the higher phases of manly character begins in
this;—in truth and modesty before the face of all
maidens; in truth and pity, or truth and reverence, to
all womanhood.

And now let me turn for a moment to you,—wives
and maidens, who are the souls of soldiers; to you,—
mothers, who have devoted your children to the great
hierarchy of war. Let me ask you to consider what
part you have to take for the aid of those who love you;
for if you fail in your part they cannot fulfil theirs; such
absolute helpmates you are that no man can stand
without that help, nor labour in his own strength.

I know your hearts, and that the truth of them never
fails when an hour of trial comes which you recognise for
such. But you know not when the hour of trial first
finds you, nor when it verily finds you. You imagine
that you are only called upon to wait and to suffer; to
surrender and to mourn. You know that you must not
weaken the hearts of your husbands and lovers, even by
the one fear of which those hearts are capable,—the
fear of parting from you, or of causing you grief.
Through weary years of separation; through fearful
expectancies of unknown fate; through the tenfold
bitterness of the sorrow which might so easily have been
joy, and the tenfold yearning for glorious life struck down
in its prime;—through all these agonies you fail not,

and never will fail.   But your trial is not in these.   To
be heroic in danger is little;—you are Englishwomen.
To be heroic in change and sway of fortune is little;—
for do you not love?   To be patient through the great
chasm and pause of loss is little;—for do you not still
love in heaven?   But to be heroic in happiness; to
bear yourselves gravely and righteously in the dazzling
of the sunshine of morning; not to forget the God in
whom you trust, when He gives you most; not to fail
those who trust you, when they seem to need you least;
this is the difficult fortitude.   It is not in the pining of
absence, not in the peril of battle, not in the wasting of
sickness, that your prayer should be most passionate,
or your guardianship most tender.   Pray, mothers and
maidens, for your young soldiers in the bloom of their
pride; pray for them, while the only dangers round them
are in their own wayward wills; watch you, and pray,
when they have to face, not death, but temptation.   But
it is this fortitude also for which there is the crowning
reward.   Believe me, the whole course and character of
your lovers' lives is in your hands; what you would have
them be, they shall be, if you not only desire to have
them so, but deserve to have them so; for they are but
mirrors in which you will see yourselves imaged.   If you
are frivolous, they will be so also; if you have no understanding of the scope of their duty, they also will forget
it; they will listen,—they *can* listen,—to no other interpretation of it than that uttered from your lips.   Bid
them be brave;—they will be brave for you: bid them
be cowards;—and how noble soever they be;—they will
quail for you.   Bid them be wise, and they will be wise
for you; mock at their counsel, they will be fools for
you: such and so absolute is your rule over them.
You fancy, perhaps, as you have been told so often,
that a wife's rule should only be over her husband's
house, not over his mind.   Ah, no! the true rule is just
the reverse of that; a true wife, in her husband's house,
is his servant; it is in his heart that she is queen.   What-

ever of best he can conceive, it is her part to be; whatever of highest he can hope, it is hers to promise; all that is dark in him she must purge into purity; all that is failing in him she must strengthen into truth: from her, through all the world's clamour, he must win his praise; in her, through all the world's warfare, he must find his peace.

And, now, but one word more. You may wonder, perhaps, that I have spoken all this night in praise of war. Yet, truly, if it might be, I, for one, would fain join in the cadence of hammer-strokes that should beat swords into ploughshares: and that this cannot be, is not the fault of us men. It is *your* fault. Wholly yours. Only by your command, or by your permission, can any contest take place among us. And the real, final, reason for all the poverty, misery, and rage of battle, throughout Europe, is simply that you women, however good, however religious, however self-sacrificing for those whom you love, are too selfish and too thoughtless to take pains for any creature out of your own immediate circles. You fancy that you are sorry for the pain of others. Now I just tell you this, that if the usual course of war, instead of unroofing peasants' houses, and ravaging peasants' fields, merely broke the china upon your own drawing-room tables, no war in civilised countries would last a week. I tell you more, that at whatever moment you chose to put a period to war, you could do it with less trouble than you take any day to go out to dinner. You know, or at least you might know if you would think, that every battle you hear of has made many widows and orphans. We have, none of us, heart enough truly to mourn with these. But at least we might put on the outer symbols of mourning with them. Let but every Christian lady who has conscience toward God, vow that she will mourn, at least outwardly, for His killed creatures. Your praying is useless, and your churchgoing mere mockery of God, if you have not plain obedience in you enough for this.   Let every lady in the upper classes of civilised Europe simply vow that, while any cruel war proceeds, she will wear *black ;*—a mute's black,—with no jewel, no ornament, no excuse for, or evasion into, prettiness—I tell you again, no war would last a week.

And lastly.   You women of England are all now shrieking with one voice,—you and your clergymen together,—because you hear of your Bibles being attacked.   If you choose to obey your Bibles, you will never care who attacks them.   It is just because you never fulfil a single downright precept of the Book, that you are so careful for its credit: and just because you don't care to obey its whole words, that you are so particular about the letters of them.   The Bible tells you to dress plainly,—and you are mad for finery; the Bible tells you to have pity on the poor,—and you crush them under your carriage wheels; the Bible tells you to do judgment and justice,—and you do not know, nor care to know, so much as what the Bible word "justice" means.   Do but learn so much of God's truth as that comes to; know what He means when He tells you to be just: and teach your sons, that their bravery is but a fool's boast, and their deeds but a fire-brand's tossing, unless they are indeed Just men, and Perfect in the Fear of God;—and you will soon have no more war, unless it be indeed such as is willed by Him, of whom, though Prince of Peace, it is also written, "In Righteousness He doth judge, and make war."

THE CESTUS OF AGLAIA

THE CESTUS OF AGLAIA

" Ποικίλον, ᾧ ἔνι πάντα τετεύχαται; οὐδέ σέ φημὶ
"Απρηκτόν γε νέεσθαι, ὅ, τι φρεσὶ σῇσι μενοινᾷς."

PREFATORY

NOT many months ago, a friend, whose familiarity
with both living and past schools of Art rendered his
opinion of great authority, said casually to me in the
course of talk, " I believe we have now as able painters
as ever lived; but they never paint as good pictures
as were once painted." That was the substance of
his saying; I forget the exact words, but their tenor
surprised me, and I have thought much of them since.
Without pressing the statement too far, or examining
it with an unintended strictness, this I believe to be at
all events true, that we have men among us, now in
Europe, who might have been noble painters, and are
not; men whose doings are altogether as wonderful in
skill, as inexhaustible in fancy, as the work of the really
great painters; and yet these doings of theirs are not
great. Shall I write the commonplace that rings in
sequence in my ear, and draws on my hand—" are not
Great, for they are not (in the broad human and ethical
sense) Good?" I write it, and ask forgiveness for the
truism, with its implied uncharitableness of blame;
for this trite thing is ill understood and little thought
upon by any of us, and the implied blame is divided
among us all; only let me at once partly modify it,
and partly define.

H

In one sense, modern Art has more goodness in it than ever Art had before. Its kindly spirit, its quick sympathy with pure domestic and social feeling, the occasional seriousness of its instructive purpose, and its honest effort to grasp the reality of conceived scenes, are all eminently " good," as compared with the inane picturesqueness and conventional piety of many among the old masters. Such domestic painting, for instance, as Richter's in Germany, Edward Frere's in France, and Hook's in England, together with such historical and ideal work as—perhaps the reader would be offended with me were I to set down the several names that occur to me here, so I will set down one only, and say—as that of Paul de la Roche; such work, I repeat, as these men have done, or are doing, is entirely good in its influence on the public mind; and may, in thankful exultation, be compared with the renderings of besotted, vicious, and vulgar human life perpetrated by Dutch painters, or with the deathful formalism and fallacy of what was once called " Historical Art." Also, this gentleness and veracity of theirs, being in part communicable, are gradually learned, though in a somewhat servile manner, yet not without a sincere sympathy, by many inferior painters, so that our exhibitions and currently popular books are full of very lovely and pathetic ideas, expressed with a care, and appealing to an interest, quite unknown in past times. I will take two instances of merely average power, as more illustrative of what I mean than any more singular and distinguished work could be. Last year, in the British Institution, there were two pictures by the same painter, one of a domestic, the other of a sacred subject. I will say nothing of the way in which they were painted; it may have been bad, or good, or neither: it is not to my point. I wish to direct attention only to the conception of them. One, " Cradled in his Calling," was of a fisherman and his

wife, and helpful grown-up son, and helpless new-
born little one; the two men carrying the young child
up from the shore, rocking it between them in the wet
net for a hammock, the mother looking on joyously,
and the baby laughing. The thought was pretty and
good, and one might go on dreaming over it long—
not unprofitably. But the second picture was more
interesting. I describe it only in the circumstances
of the invented scene—sunset after the crucifixion.
The bodies have been taken away, and the crosses are
left lying on the broken earth; a group of children
have strayed up the hill, and stopped beside them in
such shadowy awe as is possible to childhood, and they
have picked up one or two of the drawn nails to feel
how sharp they are. Meantime a girl with her little
brother—goat-herds both—have been watering their
flock at Kidron, and are driving it home. The girl,
strong in grace and honour of youth, carrying her
pitcher of water on her erect head, has gone on past
the place steadily, minding her flock; but her little
curly-headed brother, with cheeks of burning Eastern
brown, has lingered behind to look, and is feeling the
point of one of the nails, held in another child's hand.
A lovely little kid of the goats has stayed behind to
keep him company, and is amusing itself by jumping
backwards and forwards over an arm of the cross.
The sister looks back, and, wondering what he can
have stopped in that dreadful place for, waves her
hand for the little boy to come away.

I have no hesitation in saying that, as compared
with the ancient and stereotyped conceptions of the
" Taking down from the Cross," there is a living feeling
in that picture which is of great price. It may perhaps
be weak, nay, even superficial, or untenable—that will
depend on the other conditions of character out of
which it springs—but, so far as it reaches, it is pure
and good; and we may gain more by looking thought-
fully at such a picture than at any even of the least

formal types of the work of older schools. It would
be unfair to compare it with first-rate, or even approximately first-rate designs; but even accepting such
unjust terms, put it beside Rembrandt's ghastly white
sheet, laid over the two poles at the Cross-foot, and see
which has most good in it for you of any communicable
kind.

I trust, then, that I fully admit whatever may, on
due deliberation, be alleged in favour of modern Art.
Nay, I have heretofore asserted more for some modern
Art than others were disposed to admit, nor do I with-
draw one word from such assertion. But when all
has been said and granted that may be, there remains
this painful fact to be dealt with,—the consciousness,
namely, both in living artists themselves and in us
their admirers, that something, and that not a little,
is wrong with us; that they, relentlessly examined,
could not say they thoroughly knew how to paint,
and that we, relentlessly examined, could not say we
thoroughly know how to judge. The best of our
painters will look a little to us, the beholders, for
confirmation of his having done well. We, appealed
to, look to each other to see what we ought to say.
If we venture to find fault, however submissively,
the artist will probably feel a little uncomfortable: he
will by no means venture to meet us with a serenely
crushing, " Sir, it cannot be better done," in the manner
of Albert Durer. And yet, if it could not be better
done, he, of all men, should know that best, nor fear
to say so; it is good for himself, and for us, that he
should assert that, if he knows that. The last time
my dear old friend William Hunt came to see me, I
took down one of his early drawings for him to see
(three blue plums and one amber one, and two nuts).
So he looked at it, happily, for a minute or two, and
then said, " Well, it's very nice, isn't it? I did not
think I could have done so well." The saying was
entirely right, exquisitely modest and true; only I fear

he would not have had the courage to maintain that
his drawing was good, if anybody had been there to
say otherwise. Still, having done well, he knew it;
and what is more, no man ever does do well without
knowing it: he may not know *how* well, nor be conscious
of the best of his own qualities; nor measure, or care
to measure, the relation of his power to that of other
men, but he will know that what he has done is, in
an intended, accomplished, and ascertainable degree,
good. Every able and honest workman, as he wins
a right to rest, so he wins a right to approval,—his own
if no one's beside; nay, his only true rest *is* in the calm
consciousness that the thing has been honourably
done—συνείδησις ὅτι καλόν.

I do not use the Greek words in pedantry, I want them
for future service and interpretation; no English words,
nor any of any other language, would do as well. For
I mean to try to show, and believe I *can* show, that a
simple and sure conviction of our having done rightly
is not only an attainable, but a necessary seal and sign
of our having so done; and that the doing well or
rightly, and ill or wrongly, are both conditions of the
whole being of each person, coming of a nature in him
which affects all things that he may do, from the least
to the greatest, according to the noble old phrase for the
conquering rightness, of " integrity," " wholeness," or
" wholesomeness." So that when we do external things
(that are our business) ill, it is a sign that internal, and,
in fact, that all things, are ill with us; and when we do
external things well, it is a sign that internal, and all
things, are well with us. And I believe there are two
principal adversities to this wholesomeness of work, and
to all else that issues out of wholeness of inner character,
with which we have in these days specially to contend.
The first is the variety of Art round us, tempting us to
thoughtless imitation; the second our own want of
belief in the existence of a rule of right.

I. I say the first is the variety of Art around us.

No man can pursue his own track in peace, nor obtain consistent guidance, if doubtful of his track. All places are full of inconsistent example, all mouths of contradictory advice, all prospects of opposite temptations.

The young artist sees myriads of things he would like to do, but cannot learn from their authors how they were done, nor choose decisively any method which he may follow with the accuracy and confidence necessary to success. He is not even sure if his thoughts are his own; for the whole atmosphere round him is full of floating suggestion: those which are his own he cannot keep pure, for he breathes a dust of decayed ideas, wreck of the souls of dead nations, driven by contrary winds. He may stiffen himself (and all the worse for him) into an iron self-will, but if the iron has any magnetism in it, he cannot pass a day without finding himself, at the end of it, instead of sharpened or tempered, covered with a ragged fringe of iron filings. If there be anything better than iron—living wood fibre—in him, he cannot be allowed any natural growth, but gets hacked in every extremity, and bossed over with lumps of frozen clay;—grafts of incongruous blossom that will never set; while some even recognise no need of knife or clay (though both are good in a gardener's hand), but deck themselves out with incongruous glittering, like a Christmas-tree. Even were the style chosen true to his own nature, and persisted in, there is harm in the very eminence of the models set before him at the beginning of his career. If he feels their power, they make him restless and impatient, it may be despondent, it may be madly and fruitlessly ambitious. If he does not feel it, he s sure to be struck by what is weakest or slightest of their peculiar qualities; fancies that *this* is what they are praised for; tries to catch the trick of it; and whatever easy vice or mechanical habit the master may have been betrayed or warped into, the unhappy pupil watches and adopts, triumphant in its ease:—has not sense to steal the peacock's feather, but imitates its voice.   Better for him, far better, never to have seen what had been accomplished by others, but to have gained gradually his own quiet way, or at least with his guide only a step in advance of him, and the lantern low on the difficult path.   Better even, it has lately seemed, to be guideless and lightless; fortunate those who by desolate effort, trying hither and thither, have groped their way to some independent power.   So, from Cornish rock, from St. Giles's Lane, from Thames mud-shore, you get your Prout, your Hunt, your Turner; not, indeed, any of them well able to spell English, nor taught so much of their own business as to lay a colour safely; but yet at last, or first, doing somehow some-thing, wholly ineffective on the national mind, yet real, and valued at last after they are dead, in money;—valued otherwise not even at so much as the space of dead brick wall it would cover; their work being left for years packed in parcels at the National Gallery, or hung conclusively out of sight under the shadowy iron vaults of Kensington.   The men themselves, quite inarticulate, determine nothing of their Art, interpret nothing of their own minds; teach perhaps a trick or two of their stage business in early life—as for instance, that it is good where there is much black to break it with white, and where there is much white to break it with black, etc., etc.; in later life remain silent alto-gether, or speak only in despair (fretful or patient according to their character); one who might have been among the best of them, the last we heard of, finding refuge for an entirely honest heart from a world which declares honesty to be impossible, only in a madness nearly as sorrowful as its own;—the religious madness which makes a beautiful soul ludicrous and ineffectual; and so passes away, bequeathing for our inheritance from its true and strong life, a pretty song about a tiger, another about a bird-cage, two or three golden couplets, which no one will ever take the trouble to understand,—the spiritual portrait of the ghost of a flea,—and the critical opinion that "the unorganised blots of Rubens and Titian are not Art." Which opinion the public mind perhaps not boldly indorsing, is yet incapable of pronouncing adversely to it, that the said blots of Titian and Rubens *are* Art, perceiving for itself little good in them, and hanging *them* also well out of its way, at tops of walls (Titian's portrait of Charles V. at Munich, for example; Tintoret's Susannah and Veronese's Magdalen, in the Louvre), that it may have room and readiness for what may be generally termed "railroad work," bearing on matters more immediately in hand; said public looking to the present pleasure of its fancy, and the portraiture of itself in official and otherwise imposing or entertaining circumstances, as the only "Right" cognisable by it.

II. And this is a deeper source of evil, by far, than the former one, for though it is ill for us to strain towards a right for which we have never ripened, it is worse for us to believe in no right at all. "Anything," we say, "that a clever man can do to amuse us is good; what does not amuse us we do not want. Taste is assuredly a frivolous, apparently a dangerous gift; vicious persons and vicious nations have it; we are a practical people, content to know what we like, wise in not liking it too much, and when tired of it, wise in getting something we like better. Painting is of course an agreeable ornamental Art, maintaining a number of persons respectably, deserving therefore encouragement, and getting it pecuniarily, to an hitherto unheard of extent. What would you have more?" This is, I believe, very nearly our Art-creed. The fact being (very ascertainably by any one who will take the trouble to examine the matter) that there is a cultivated Art among all great nations, inevitably necessary to them as the fulfilment of one part of their human nature. None but savage nations are without Art, and civilised nations

who do their Art ill, do it because there is something
deeply wrong at their hearts. They paint badly as a
paralysed man stammers, because his life is touched
somewhere within; when the deeper life is full in
a people, they speak clearly and rightly; paint clearly
and rightly; think clearly and rightly. There is some
reverse effect, but very little. Good pictures do not
teach a nation; they are the signs of its having been
taught. Good thoughts do not form a nation; it must
be formed before it can think them. Let it once decay
at the heart, and its good work and good thoughts will
become subtle luxury and aimless sophism; and it and
they will perish together.

It is my purpose, therefore, in some subsequent
papers, with such help as I may anywise receive, to try
if there may not be determined some of the simplest
laws which are indeed binding in Art practice and
judgment.

Beginning with elementary principle, and proceeding upwards as far as guiding laws are discernible,
I hope to show, that if we do not yet know them, there
are at least such laws to be known, and that it is of a
deep and intimate importance to any people, especially
to the English at this time, that their children should
be sincerely taught whatever arts they learn, and in
riper age become capable of a just choice and wise
pleasure in the accomplished works of the artist. But
I earnestly ask for help in this task. It is one which
can only come to good issue by the consent and aid of
many thinkers; and I would invite debate on the subject of each paper, together with brief and clear statements of consent or objection, with name of consenter
or objector: so that after courteous discussion had, and
due correction of the original statement, we may get
something at least set down, as harmoniously believed
by such and such known artists. If nothing can thus be
determined, at last the manner and variety of dissent

will show whether it is owing to the nature of the subject, or to the impossibility, under present circumstances, that different persons should approach it from similar points of view; and the inquiry, whatever its immediate issue, cannot be ultimately fruitless.

CHAPTER I

OUR knowledge of human labour, if intimate enough, will, I think, mass it for the most part into two kinds— mining and moulding; the labour that seeks for things, and the labour that shapes them. Of these the last should be always orderly, for we ought to have some conception of the whole of what we have to make, before we try to make any part of it: but the labour of seeking must be often methodless, following the veins of the mine as they branch, or trying for them where they are broken. And the mine, which we would now open into the souls of men, as they govern the mysteries of their handicrafts, being rent into many dark and divided ways, it is not possible to map our work beforehand, or resolve on its directions. We will not attempt to bind ourselves to any methodical treatment of our subject, but will get at the truths of it here and there, as they seem extricable: only, though we cannot know to what depth we may have to dig, let us know clearly what we are digging for. We desire to find by what rule some Art is called good, and other Art bad: we desire to find the conditions of character in the artist which are essentially connected with the goodness of his work: we desire to find what are the methods of practice which form this character, or corrupt it; and finally, how the formation or corruption of this character is connected with the general prosperity of nations.

And all this we want to learn practically: not for mere pleasant speculation on things that have been; but for instant direction of those that are yet to be. My first object is to get at some fixed principles for the teaching of Art to our youth; and I am about to ask, of all who may be able to give me a serviceable answer, and with and for all who are anxious for such answer, what arts should be generally taught to the English boy and girl,—by what methods,—and to what ends? How well, or how imperfectly, our youth of the higher classes should be disciplined in the practice of music and painting?—how far, among the lower classes, exercise in certain mechanical arts might become a part of their school life?—how far, in the adult life of this nation, the Fine Arts may advisably supersede or regulate the mechanical Arts? Plain questions these, enough! clearly also important ones; and, as clearly, boundless ones—mountainous—infinite in contents—only to be mined into in a scrambling manner by poor enquirers, as their present tools and sight may serve.

I have often been accused of dogmatism, and confess to the holding strong opinions on some matters; but I tell the reader in sincerity, and entreat him in sincerity to believe, that I do not think myself able to dictate anything positive respecting questions of this magnitude. The one thing I am sure of is, the need of some form of dictation; or, where that is as yet impossible, at least of consistent experiment, for the just solution of doubts which present themselves every day in more significant and more impatient temper of interrogation.

Here is one, for instance, lying at the base of all the rest—namely, what may be the real dignity of mechanical Art itself? I cannot express the amazed awe, the crushed humility—with which I sometimes watch a locomotive take its breath at a railway station, and think what work there is in its bars and wheels, and what manner of men they must be who dig brown ironstone out of the ground, and forge it into THAT! What assemblage of accurate and mighty faculties in them; more than fleshly power over melting crag and coiling fire, fettered, and finessed at last into the precision of watch-making;

Titanian hammer-strokes beating, out of lava, these
glittering cylinders and timely-respondent valves, and
fine ribbed rods, which touch each other as a serpent
writhes, in noiseless gliding, and omnipotence of grasp;
infinitely complex anatomy of active steel, compared
with which the skeleton of a living creature would seem,
to a careless observer, clumsy and vile—a mere morbid
secretion and phosphatous prop of flesh! What would
the men who thought out this,—who beat it out, who
touched it into its polished calm of power, who set it
to its appointed task, and triumphantly saw it fulfil
this task to the utmost of their will,—feel or think
about this weak hand of mine, timidly leading a little
stain of water-colour, which I cannot manage, into an
imperfect shadow of something else,—mere failure in
every motion, and endless disappointment;—What, I
repeat, would these Iron-dominant Genii think of me?
and what ought I to think of them?

But as I reach this point of reverence, the unreasonable thing is sure to give a shriek as of a thousand
unanimous vultures, which leaves me shuddering in real
physical pain for some half minute following; and
assures me during slow recovery, that a people which
can endure such fluting and piping among them is not
likely soon to have its modest ear pleased by aught of
oaten stop, or pastoral song. Perhaps I am then led
on into meditation respecting the spiritual nature of the
Tenth Muse, who invented this gracious instrument,
and guides its modulation by stokers' fingers;—meditation, also, as to the influence of her invention amidst
the other parts of the Parnassian melody of English
education. Then it cannot but occur to me to enquire
how far this modern " pneuma," Steam, may be connected with other pneumatic powers talked of in that
old religious literature, of which we fight so fiercely to
keep the letters bright, and the working valves, so to
speak, in good order (while we let the steam of it all
carefully off into the cold condenser), what connection,

I say, this modern " spiritus," in its valve-directed inspiration, has with that more ancient spiritus, or warm breath, which people used to think they might be " born of." Whether, in fine, there be any such thing as an entirely human Art, with spiritual motive power, and signal as of human voice, distinct inherently from this mechanical Art, with its mechanical motive force, and signal of vulture voice. For after all, this shrieking thing, whatever the fine make of it may be, can but pull, or push, and do oxen's work, in an impetuous manner. That proud king of Assyria, who lost his reason, and ate oxen's food, would he have had much more cause for pride, if he had been allowed to spend his reason in doing oxen's work?

These things, then, I would fain consult about, and plead with the reader for his patience in council, even while we begin with the simplest practical matters; for ravelled briars of thought entangle our feet, even at our first step. We would teach a boy to draw. Well, what shall he draw?—Gods, or men, or beasts, or clouds, or leaves, or iron cylinders? Are there any gods to be drawn? any men or women worth drawing, or only worth caricaturing? What are the æsthetic laws respecting iron cylinders; and would Titian have liked them rusty, or fresh cleaned with oil and rag, to fill the place once lightened by St. George's armour? How can we begin the smallest practical business, unless we get first some whisper of answer to such questions? We may tell a boy to draw a straight line straight, and a crooked one crooked; but what else?

And it renders the dilemma, or multilemma, more embarrassing, that whatever teaching is to be had from the founders and masters of Art is quite unpractical. The first source from which we should naturally seek for guidance would, of course, be the sayings of great workmen; but a sorrowful perception presently dawns on us, that the great workmen have nothing to say! They are silent,—absolutely in proportion to their creative power. The contributions to our practical knowledge of the principles of Art, furnished by the true captains of its hosts, may, I think, be arithmetically summed by the **0** of Giotto:—the inferior teachers become didactic in the degree of their inferiority; and those who can do nothing, have always much to advise.

This however, observe, is only true of advice direct. You never, I grieve to say, get from the great men a plain answer to a plain question; still less can you entangle them in any agreeable gossip, out of which something might unawares be picked up. But of enigmatical teaching, broken signs and sullen mutterings, of which you can understand nothing, and may make anything;—of confused discourse in the work itself, about the work, as in Durer's Melencolia;—and of discourse not merely confused, but apparently unreasonable and ridiculous, about all manner of things *except* the work,—the great Egyptian and Greek artists give us much: from which, however, all that by utmost industry may be gathered, comes briefly to this,—that they have no conception of what modern men of science call the " Conservation of forces," but deduce all the force they feel in themselves, and hope for in others, from certain fountains or centres of perpetually supplied strength, to which they give various names: as, for instance, these seven following, more specially:—

1. The Spirit of Light, moral and physical, by name the " Physician-Destroyer," bearing arrows in his hand, and a lyre; pre-eminently the destroyer of human pride, and the guide of human harmony. Physically, Lord of the Sun; and a mountain Spirit, because the sun seems first to rise and set upon hills.

2. The Spirit of helpful Darkness,—of shade and rest. Night the Restorer.

3. The Spirit of Wisdom in *Conduct*, bearing, in sign of conquest over troublous and disturbing evil, the skin of the wild goat, and the head of the

slain Spirit of physical storm.   In her hand,
a weaver's shuttle, or a spear.

4. The Spirit of Wisdom in *Arrangement ;* called the
Lord or Father of Truth: throned on a four-
square cubit, with a measuring-rod in his hand,
or a potter's wheel.

5. The Spirit of Wisdom in *Adaptation ;* or of serviceable labour: the Master of human effort in its
glow; and Lord of useful fire, moral and
physical.

6. The Spirit, first of young or nascent grace, and
then of fulfilled beauty: the wife of the Lord
of labour. I have taken the two lines in
which Homer describes her girdle, for the
motto of these essays: partly in memory of
these outcast fancies of the great masters:
and partly for the sake of a meaning which
we shall find as we go on.

7. The Spirit of pure human life and gladness.
Master of wholesome vital passion; and, physically, Lord of the vine.

From these ludicrous notions of motive force, inconsistent as they are with modern physiology and organic
chemistry, we may, nevertheless, hereafter gather, in
the details of their various expression, something useful
to us.   But I grieve to say that when our provoking
teachers descend from dreams about the doings of Gods
to assertions respecting the deeds of Men, little beyond
the blankest discouragement is to be had from them.
Thus, they represent the ingenuity, and deceptive or
imitative Arts of men, under the type of a Master
who builds labyrinths, and makes images of living
creatures, for evil purposes, or for none; and pleases
himself and the people with idle jointing of toys, and
filling of them with quicksilver motion; and brings his
child to foolish, remediless catastrophe, in fancying his
father's work as good, and strong, and fit to bear sunlight, as if it had been God's work.   So, again, they

represent the foresight and kindly zeal of men by a
most rueful figure, of one chained down to a rock by the
brute force and bias and methodical hammer-stroke of
the merely practical Arts, and by the merciless Necessities or Fates of present time; and so having his very
heart torn piece by piece out of him by a vulturous
hunger and sorrow, respecting things he cannot reach,
nor prevent, nor achieve. So, again, they describe the
sentiment and pure soul-power of Man as moving the
very rocks and trees, and giving them life, by its
sympathy with them; but losing its own best-beloved
thing by mere venomous accident: and afterwards
going down to hell for it, in vain; being impatient and
unwise, though full of gentleness; and, in the issue,
after as vainly trying to teach this gentleness to others,
and to guide them out of their lower passions to sunlight of true healing Life, it drives the sensual heart of
them, and the gods that govern it, into mere and pure
frenzy of resolved rage, and gets torn to pieces by them,
and ended; only the nightingale staying by its grave
to sing. All which appearing to be anything rather
than helpful or encouraging instruction for beginners, we
shall, for the present, I think, do well to desire these
enigmatical teachers to put up their pipes and begone;
and betaking ourselves in the humblest manner to intel-
ligible business, at least set down some definite matter
for decision, to be made a first stepping-stone at the
shore of this brook of despond and difficulty.

Most masters agree (and I believe they are right) that
the first thing to be taught to any pupil, is how to draw
an outline of such things as can be outlined.

Now, there are two kinds of outline—the soft and
hard. One must be executed with a soft instrument, as
a piece of chalk or lead; and the other with some instrument producing for ultimate result a firm line of equal
darkness; as a pen with ink, or the engraving tool on
wood or metal.

And these two kinds of outline have both of them

I

their particular objects and uses, as well as their proper scale of size in work. Thus Raphael will sketch a miniature head with his pen, but always takes chalk if he draws of the size of life. So also Holbein, and generally the other strong masters.

But the black outline seems to be peculiarly that which we ought to begin to reason upon, because it is simple and open-hearted, and does not endeavour to escape into mist. A pencil line may be obscurely and undemonstrably wrong; false in a cowardly manner, and without confession; but the ink line, if it goes wrong at all, goes wrong with a will, and may be convicted at our leisure, and put to such shame as its black complexion is capable of. May we, therefore, begin with the hard line? It will lead us far, if we can come to conclusions about it.

Presuming, then, that our schoolboys are such as Coleridge would have them—*i.e.* that they are

" Innocent, steady, and wise,
And delight in the things of earth, water, and skies; "

and, above all, in a moral state in which they may be trusted with ink,—we put a pen into their hands (shall it be steel?) and a piece of smooth white paper, and something before them to draw. But what? " Nay," the reader answers, " you had surely better give them pencil first, for that may be rubbed out." Perhaps so; but I am not sure that the power of rubbing out is an advantage; at all events, we shall best discover what the pencil outline ought to be, by investigating the power of the black one, and the kind of things we can draw with it.

Suppose, for instance, my first scholar has a turn for entomology, and asks me to draw for him a wasp's leg, or its sting; having first humanely provided me with a model by pulling one off, or out. My pen must clearly be fine at the point, and my execution none of the boldest, if I comply with his request. If I decline, and he thereupon challenges me at least to draw the wasp's body, with its pretty bands of black crinoline—behold us involved instantly in the profound question of local colour! Am I to tell him he is not to draw outlines of bands or spots? How, then, shall he know a wasp's body from a bee's? I escape, for the present, by telling him the story of Dædalus and the honeycomb;—set him to draw a pattern of hexagons, and lay the question of black bands up in my mind.

The next boy, we may suppose, is a conchologist, and asks me to draw a white snail-shell for him! Veiling my consternation at the idea of having to give a lesson on the perspective of geometrical spirals, with an "austere regard of control" I pass on to the next student:—Who, bringing after him, with acclamation, all the rest of the form, requires of me, contemptuously, to "draw a horse!"

And I retreat in final discomfiture; for not only I cannot myself execute, but I have never seen, an outline, quite simply and rightly done, either of a shell or a pony; nay, not so much as of a pony's nose. At a girls' school we might perhaps take refuge in rose-buds; but these boys, with their impatient battle-cry, "my kingdom for a horse," what is to be done for them?

Well, this is what I should like to be able to do for them. To show them an enlarged black outline, nobly done, of the two sides of a coin of Tarentum, with that fiery rider kneeling, careless, on his horse's neck, and reclined on his surging dolphin, with the curled sea lapping round them; and then to convince my boys that no one (unless it were Taras's father himself, with the middle prong of his trident) could draw a horse like that, without learning;—that for poor mortals like us there must be sorrowful preparatory stages; and, having convinced them of this, set them to draw (if I had a good copy to give them) a horse's hoof, or his rib, or a vertebra of his thunder-clothed neck, or any other constructive piece of him.

Meanwhile, all this being far out of present reach, I am fain to shrink back into my snail-shell, both for shelter, and calm of pace; and ask of artists in general how the said shell, or any other simple object involving varied contour, *should* be outlined in ink?—how thick the lines should be, and how varied? My own idea of an elementary outline is that it should be unvaried; distinctly visible; not thickened towards the shaded sides of the object; not express any exaggerations of aerial perspective, nor fade at the further side of a cup as if it were the further side of a crater of a volcano; and therefore, in objects of ordinary size, show no gradation at all, unless where the real outline disappears, as in soft contours and folds. Nay, I think it may even be a question whether we ought not to resolve that the line should never gradate itself at all, but terminate quite bluntly! Albert Durer's "Cannon" furnishes a very peculiar and curious example of this entirely equal line, even to the extreme distance; being in that respect opposed to nearly all his other work, which is wrought mostly by tapering lines; and his work in general, and Holbein's, which appear to me entirely typical of rightness in use of the graver and pen, are to be considered carefully in their relation to Rembrandt's loose etching, as in the "Spotted Shell." But I do not want to press my own opinions now, even when I have been able to form them distinctly. I want to get at some unanimous expression of opinion and method; and would propose, therefore, in all modesty, this question for discussion, by such artists as will favour me with answer,[1] giving their

[1] I need not say that this enquiry can only be pursued by the help of those who will take it up good-humouredly and graciously: such help I will receive in the spirit in which it is given; entering into no controversy, but questioning further where there is doubt:—gathering all I can into focus, and passing silently by what seems at last irreconcilable.

names:—*How ought the pen to be used to outline a form
of varied contour ; and ought outline to be entirely pure,
or, even in its most elementary types, to pass into some
suggestion of shade in the inner masses ?*   For there are
no examples whatever of pure outlines by the great
masters. They are always touched or modified by
inner lines, more or less suggestive of solid form, and
they are lost, or accentuated, in certain places, not so
much in conformity with any explicable law, as in expression of the master's future purpose, or of what he
wishes immediately to note in the character of the
object. Most of them are irregular memoranda, not
systematic elementary work: of those which are sys-
tematised, the greater part are carried far beyond the
initiative stage; and Holbein's are nearly all washed
with colour: the exact degree in which he depends upon
the softening and extending his touch of ink by subsequent solution of it, being indeterminable, though
exquisitely successful. His stupendous drawings in
the British Museum (I can justly use no other term
than " stupendous," of their consummately decisive
power) furnish finer instances of this treatment than
any at Basle; but it would be very difficult to reduce
them to a definable law. Venetian outlines are rare,
except preparations on canvas, often shaded before
colouring;—while Raphael's, if not shaded, are quite
loose, and useless as examples to a beginner: so that we
are left wholly without guide as to the preparatory steps
on which we should decisively insist; and I am myself
haunted by the notion that the students were forced to
shade firmly from the very beginning, in all the greatest
schools; only we never can get hold of any beginnings,
or any weak work of those schools: whatever is bad in
them comes of decadence, not infancy.

I purpose in the next essay to enter upon quite
another part of the enquiry, so as to leave time for
the reception of communications bearing upon the

present paper: and, according to their importance, I shall ask leave still to defer our return to the subject until I have had time to reflect upon them, and to collect for public service the concurrent opinions they may contain.

CHAPTER II

" Sir, it cannot be better done."

WE will return, with the reader's permission, for a little while, to this comfortful saying of Albert Durer's, in order to find out, if we may, what Modesty is; which it will be well for painters, readers, and especially critics, to know, before going farther. What it is; or, rather, who she ıs; her fingers being among the deftest in laying the ground-threads of Aglaia's Cestus.

For this same opinion of Albert's is entertained by many other people respecting their own doings—a very prevalent opinion, indeed, I find it; and the answer itself, though, as aforesaid, not made with any crushing decision, is nevertheless often enough intimated, with delicacy, by artists of all countries, in their various dialects:—neither can it always be held an entirely modest one, as it assuredly was in the man who would often estimate a piece of his unconquerable work at only the worth of a plate of fruit, or a flask of wine—would have taken even one " fig for it," kindly offered; or given it royally for nothing, " to show his hand " to a fellow-being of his own or any other craft; as Gainsborough gave the " Boy at the Stile " for a solo on the violin. An entirely modest saying, I repeat, in him—not always in us. For Modesty is " the measuring virtue," the virtue of *modes* or limits: she is indeed said to be only the third or youngest of the children of the cardinal virtue, Temperance; and apt to be despised, being more given to arithmetic and other vulgar studies (Cinderella-like) than her elder sisters; but she is useful in the household, and arrives at great results with her yard-

135

measure and slate-pencil—a pretty little Marchande des
Modes, cutting her dress always according to the silk
(if this be the proper feminine reading of " coat according to the cloth "), so that, consulting with her carefully,
of a morning, men get to know not only their income,
but their inbeing—to know *themselves*, that is, in a
gauger's manner; round, and up and down—surface
and contents; what is in them, and what may be got
out of them; and, in fine, their entire canon of weight
and capacity. That yard-measure of Modesty's, lent
to those who will use it, is a curious musical reed, and
will go round and round waists that are slender enough,
with latent melody in every joint of it, the dark root only
being soundless, moist from the wave wherein

> " Null 'altra pianta che facesse fronda
>   O indurasse, puote aver vita." [1]

But when the little sister herself takes it in hand, to
measure things outside of us with, the joints shoot out
in an amazing manner: the four-square walls even of
celestial cities being measurable enough by that reed;
and the way pointed to them, though only to be followed,
or even seen, in the dim starlight shed down from
worlds amidst which there is no name of Measure any
more, though the reality of it always. For, indeed, to
all true modesty the necessary business is not inlook,
but outlook, and especially *up*look; it is only her
sister, Shamefacedness, who is known by the drooping
lashes;—Modesty, quite otherwise, by her large eyes
full of wonder;—for she never contemns herself, nor is
ashamed of herself, but forgets herself—at least until
she has done something worth memory. It is easy to
peep and potter about one's own deficiencies in a quite
immodest discontent; but Modesty is so pleased with
other people's doings, that she has no leisure to lament
her own; and thus, knowing the fresh feeling of contentment, unstained with thought of self, she does not fear

[1] *Purgatorio*, i. 103.

being pleased, when there is cause, with her own rightness, as with another's, saying calmly, " Be it mine, or
yours, or whose else's it may, it is no matter;—this also
is well." But the right to say such a thing depends
on continual reverence, and manifold sense of failure.
If you have known yourself to have failed, you may
trust the strange consciousness of success; if you have
faithfully loved the noble work of others, you need not
fear to speak with respect of things duly done, of your
own.

But the principal good that comes of arts being
followed in this reverent feeling, is vitally manifest in the
associative conditions of it. Men who know their place
can take it, and keep it, be it low or high, contentedly
and firmly; neither yielding nor grasping: and the
harmony of hand and thought follows, rendering all
great deeds of Art possible—deeds in which the souls of
men meet like the window jewels of Aladdin's palace,
the little gems and the large all equally pure, needing
no cement but the fitting of facets; while the associative work of immodest men is all jointless, and astir with
wormy ambition; putridly dissolute, and for ever on the
crawl: so that if it come together for a time, it can only
be by metamorphism through flash of volcanic fire out
of the vale of Siddim, vitrifying the clay of it, and
fastening the slime, only to end in wilder scattering,
according to the fate of those oldest, mightiest, im-
modestest of builders, of whom it is told in scorn,
" They had brick for stone, and slime had they for
mortar."

The first function of Modesty, then, being this recognition of Place, her second is the recognition of Law,
and delight in it, for the sake of law itself, whether her
part be to assert it, or obey. For as it belongs to all
immodesty to defy or deny law, and assert privilege
and licence according to its own pleasure (it being therefore rightly called " in*solent*," that is, " custom break-
ing," violating some usual and appointed order to

attain for itself greater forwardness or power), so it is
the habit of all modesty to love the constancy and
" *solem*nity," or literally " accustomedness," of law,
seeking first what are the solemn, appointed, inviolable
customs and general orders of nature, and of the Master
of nature, touching the matter in hand; and striving
to put itself, as habitually, and inviolably, in compli-
ance with them.   Out of which habit, once established,
arises what is rightly called " conscience," not " science "
merely, but " with-science," a science " with us," such
as only modest creatures can have—with, or within
them,—and within all creation besides, every member of
it, strong or weak, witnessing together, and joining in
the happy consciousness that each one's work is good;
the bee also being profoundly of that opinion; and the
lark; and the swallow, in that noisy, but modestly
upside-down, Babel of hers under the eaves, with its
unvolcanic slime for mortar; and the two ants who are
asking of each other at the turn of that little ant's-foot-
worn path through the moss, " lor via e lor fortuna; "
and the builders also, who built yonder pile of cloud-
marble in the west, and the Gilder who gilded it, and is
gone down, behind it.

But I think we shall better understand what we ought
of the nature of Modesty, and her opposite, by taking a
simple instance of both, in the practice of that art of
music, which the wisest of men have agreed in thinking
the first element of education: only I must ask the
reader's patience with me through a parenthesis.

Among the foremost men whose power has had to
assert itself, though with conquest, yet with countless
loss, through all those peculiar English disadvantages
of circumstance of which I spoke in the prefatory
chapter, are assuredly to be ranked together, both for
honour and for mourning, Thomas Bewick, and George
Cruikshank.   There is, however, less cause for regret
in the instance of Bewick.   We may understand that
it was well for us once to see what an entirely powerful

painter's genius, and an entirely keen and true man's temper, could achieve together, unhelped, but also unharmed, among the black banks and wolds of Tyne. But the genius of Cruikshank has been cast away in an utterly ghastly and lamentable manner: his superb line-work, worthy of any class of subject, and his powers of conception and composition, of which I cannot venture to estimate the range in their degraded application, having been condemned, by his fate, to be spent either in rude jesting, or in vain war with conditions of vice too low alike for record or rebuke, among the dregs of the British populace. Yet perhaps I am wrong in regretting even this: it may be an appointed lesson for futurity, that the art of the best English etcher in the nineteenth century, spent on illustrations of the lives of burglars and drunkards, should one day be seen in museums beneath Greek vases fretted with drawings of the wars of Troy, or side by side with Durer's " Knight and Death."

Be that as it may, I am at present glad to be able to refer to one of these perpetuations, by his strong hand, of such human character as our faultless British constitution occasionally produces, in out-of-the-way corners. It is among his illustrations of the Irish Rebellion, and represents the pillage and destruction of a gentleman's house by the mob. They have made a heap in the drawing-room of the furniture and books, to set first fire to; and are tearing up the floor for its more easily kindled planks: the less busily-disposed meanwhile hacking round in rage, with axes; and smashing what they can with butt-ends of guns. I do not care to follow with words the ghastly truth of the picture into its detail; but the most expressive incident of the whole, and the one immediately to my purpose, is this, that one fellow has sat himself at the piano, on which, hitting down fiercely with his clenched fists, he plays, grinning, such tune as may be so producible, to which melody two of his companions, flourishing

knotted sticks, dance, after their manner, on the top
of the instrument.

I think we have in this conception as perfect an
instance as we require of the lowest supposable phase
of immodest or licentious art in music; the "inner
consciousness of good" being dim, even in the musician
and his audience, and wholly unsympathised with, and
unacknowledged, by the Delphian, Vestal, and all other
prophetic and cosmic powers. This represented scene
came into my mind suddenly, one evening, a few weeks
ago, in contrast with another which I was watching
in its reality, namely, a group of gentle school-girls
leaning over Mr. Charles Hallé as he was playing a
variation on "Home, Sweet Home." They had sustained with unwonted courage the glance of subdued
indignation with which, having just closed a rippling
melody of Sebastian Bach's (much like what one
might fancy the singing of nightingales would be if they
fed on honey instead of flies), he turned to the slight,
popular air. But they had their own associations
with it, and besought for it, and obtained it: and
pressed close, at first, in vain, to see what no glance
could follow, the traversing of the fingers. They soon
thought no more of seeing. The wet eyes, round-open,
and the little scarlet upper lips, lifted and drawn
slightly together in passionate glow of utter wonder,
became picture-like, porcelain-like, in motionless joy,
as the sweet multitude of low notes fell in their timely
infinities, like summer rain. Only La Robbia himself
(nor even he, unless with tenderer use of colour than
is usual in his work) could have rendered some image of
that listening.

But if the reader can give due vitality in his fancy
to these two scenes, he will have in them representative
types, clear enough for all future purpose, of the several
agencies of debased and perfect Art. And the interval
may easily and continuously be filled by mediate gradations. Between the entirely immodest, unmeasured,

and (in evil sense) unmannered, execution with the
Fist, and the entirely modest, measured, and (in the
noblest sense) mannered or moral'd execution with
the Finger;—between the impatient and unpractised
doing, containing in itself the witness of lasting impatience and idleness through all previous life, and the
patient and practised doing, containing in itself the
witness of self-restraint and unwearied toil through
all previous life;—between the expressed subject and
sentiment of home violation, and the expressed subject
and sentiment of home love;—between the sympathy
of audience given in irreverent and contemptuous rage,
joyless as tne rabidness of a dog, and the sympathy
of audience given in an almost appalled humility of
intense, rapturous, and yet entirely reasoning and reasonable pleasure;—between these two limits of octave
the reader will find he can class, according to their
modesty, usefulness, and grace or becomingness, all
other modes of musical art. For although purity of
purpose and fineness of execution by no means go
together, degree to degree (since fine, and indeed all
but the finest, work is often spent in the most wanton
purpose—as in all our modern opera—and the rudest
execution is again often joined with purest purpose, as
in a mother's song to her child), still the entire accomplishment of music is only in the union of both. For
the difference between that "all but" finest and
"finest" is an infinite one; and besides this, we shall
find that however the power of the performer, once
attained, may be afterwards misdirected, in slavery
to popular passion or childishness, and spend itself,
at its sweetest, in idle melodies, cold and ephemeral
(like Michael Angelo's snow statue in the other art),
or else in vicious difficulty and miserable noise—
crackling of thorns under the pot of public sensuality—
still the attainment of this power, and the maintenance
of it, involve always in the executant some virtue or
courage of high kind; the understanding of which,

and of the difference between the discipline which
develops it and the disorderly efforts of the amateur,
it will be one of our first businesses to estimate rightly.
And though not indeed by degree to degree, yet in
essential relation (as of winds to waves, the one being
always the true cause of the other, though they are not
necessarily of equal force at the same time), we shall
find vice in its varieties, with Art-failure, and virtue
in its varieties, with Art-success, fall and rise together:
the peasant girl's song at her spinning-wheel, the
peasant-labourer's " to the oaks and rills,"—domestic
music, feebly yet sensitively skilful,—music for the
multitude, of beneficent, or of traitorous power,—
dance-melodies, pure and orderly, or foul and frantic,—
march-music, blatant in mere fever of animal pugnacity,
or majestic with force of national duty and memory,—
song-music, reckless, sensual, sickly, slovenly, forgetful
even of the foolish words it effaces with foolish noise,—
or thoughtful, sacred, healthful, artful, for ever sanctifying noble thought with separately distinguished loveliness of belonging sound,—all these families and gradations of good or evil, however mingled, follow, in so
far as they are good, one constant law of virtue (or
" life-strength," which is the literal meaning of the
word, and its intended one, in wise men's mouths), and
in so far as they are evil, are evil by outlawry and
unvirtue, or death-weakness. Then, passing wholly
beyond the domain of death, we may still imagine the
ascendant nobleness of the art, through all the con-
cordant life of incorrupt creatures, and a continually
deeper harmony of " *puissant* words and murmurs
made to bless; " until we reach—

> " The undisturbed song of pure consent,
> Aye sung before the sapphire-coloured throne."

And so far as the sister arts can be conceived to have
place or office, their virtues are subject to a law absolutely the same as that of music, only extending its

authority into more various conditions, owing to the introduction of a distinctly representative and historical power, which acts under logical as well as mathematical restrictions, and is capable of endlessly changeful fault, fallacy, and defeat, as well as of endlessly manifold victory.

To the discernment of this law we will now address ourselves slowly, beginning with the consideration of little things, and of easily definable virtues. And since Patience is the pioneer of all the others, I shall endeavour in the next paper to show how that modest virtue has been either held of no account, or else set to vilest work in our modern Art-schools; and what harm has resulted from such disdain, or such employment of her.

CHAPTER III

"Dame Paciencĕ sitting there I fonde,
    With facĕ pale, upon an hill of sonde."

As I try to summon this vision of Chaucer's into definiteness, and as it fades before me, and reappears, like the image of Piccarda in the moon, there mingles with it another;—the image of an Italian child, lying, she also, upon a hill of sand, by Eridanus' side; a vision which has never quite left me since I saw it. A girl of ten or twelve, it might be; one of the children to whom there has never been any other lesson taught than that of patience:—patience of famine and thirst; patience of heat and cold; patience of fierce word and sullen blow; patience of changeless fate and giftless time. She was lying with her arms thrown back over her head, all languid and lax, on an earth-heap by the river-side, (the softness of the dust being the only softness she had ever known), in the southern suburb of Turin, one golden afternoon in August, years ago. She had been at play, after her fashion, with other patient children, and had thrown herself down to rest, full in the sun, like a lizard. The sand was mixed with the draggled locks of her black hair, and some of it sprinkled over her face and body, in an "ashes to ashes" kind of way;—a few black rags about her loins, but her limbs nearly bare, and her little breasts, scarce dimpled yet, —white,—marble-like—but, as wasted marble, thin with the scorching and the rains of Time. So she lay, motionless; black and white by the shore in the sun; the yellow light flickering back upon her from the passing eddies of the river, and burning down on her from

the west.   So she lay, like a dead Niobid; it seemed as
if the Sun-God, as he sank towards grey Viso, (who stood
pale in the south-west, and pyramidal as a tomb), had
been wroth with Italy for numbering her children too
carefully, and slain this little one.   Black and white
she lay, all breathless, in a sufficiently pictorial manner:
the gardens of the Villa Regina gleamed beyond, graceful with laurel-grove and labyrinthine terrace;   and
folds of purple mountain were drawn afar, for curtains
round her little dusty bed.   Pictorial enough, I repeat;
and yet I might not now have remembered her, so
as to find her figure mingling, against my will, with
other images, but for her manner of " revival."   For
one of her playmates coming near, cast some word at
her which angered her; and she rose—" en ego, victa
situ "—she rose, with a single spring, like a snake; one
hardly saw the motion; and with a shriek so shrill that
I put my hands upon my ears; and so uttered herself,
indignant and vengeful, with words of justice,—Alecto
standing by, satisfied, teaching her acute, articulate
syllables, and adding her own voice to carry them
thrilling through the blue laurel shadows.   And having
spoken, she went her way, wearily: and I passed by
on the other side, meditating, with such Levitical pro-
priety as a respectable person should, on the asp-like
Passion, following the sorrowful Patience; and on the
way in which the saying, " Dust shalt thou eat all thy
days " has been confusedly fulfilled, first by much pro-
vision of human dust for the meat of what Keats calls
" human serpentry; " and last, by gathering the Consumed and Consumer into dust together, for the meat
of the death spirit, or serpent Apap.   Neither could I,
for long, get rid of the thought of this strange dust-
manufacture under the mill-stones, as it were, of Death;
and of the two colours of the grain, discriminate beneath,
though indiscriminately cast into the hopper.   For
indeed some of it seems only to be made whiter for its
patience, and becomes kneadable into spiced bread,

where they sell in Babylonian shops " slaves, and souls
of men ; " but other some runs dark from under the
mill-stones ; a little sulphurous and nitrous foam being
mingled in the conception of it ; and is ominously
stored up in magazines near river-embankments ; patient
enough—for the present.

But it is provoking to me that the image of this child
mingles itself now with Chaucer's ; for I should like
truly to know what Chaucer means by his sand-hill.
Not but that this is just one of those enigmatical pieces
of teaching which we have made up our minds not to be
troubled with, since it may evidently mean just what
we like. Sometimes I would fain have it to mean the
ghostly sand of the horologe of the world : and I think
that the pale figure is seated on the recording heap,
which rises slowly, and ebbs in giddiness, and flows
again, and rises, tottering ; and still she sees, falling
beside her, the never-ending stream of phantom sand.
Sometimes I like to think that she is seated on the sand
because she is herself the Spirit of Staying, and victor
over all things that pass and change ;—quicksand of the
desert in moving pillar ; quicksand of the sea in moving
floor ; roofless all, and unabiding, but she abiding ;—
to herself, her home. And sometimes I think, though
I do not like to think (neither did Chaucer mean this,
for he always meant the lovely thing first, not the low
one), that she is seated on her sand-heap as the only
treasure to be gained by human toil ; and that the
little ant-hill, where the best of us creep to and fro,
bears to angelic eyes, in the patientest gathering of its
galleries, only the aspect of a little heap of dust ; while
for the worst of us, the heap, still lower by the levelling
of those winged surveyors, is high enough, nevertheless,
to overhang, and at last to close in judgment, on the
seventh day, over the journeyers to the fortunate
Islands ; while to their dying eyes, through the mirage,
" the city sparkles like a grain of salt."

But of course it does not in the least matter what it

means. All that matters specially to us in Chaucer's vision, is that, next to Patience, (as the reader will find by looking at the context in the " Assembly of Foules ") were " Beheste " and " Art ; "—Promise, that is, and Art: and that, although these visionary powers are here waiting only in one of the outer courts of Love, and the intended patience is here only the long-suffering of love; and the intended beheste, its promise; and the intended art, its cunning,—the same powers companion each other necessarily in the courts and ante-chambers of every triumphal home of man. I say triumphal home, for, indeed, triumphal *arches* which you pass under, are but foolish things, and may be nailed together any day, out of pasteboard and filched laurel; but triumphal *doors*, which you can enter in at, with living laurel crowning the Lares, are not so easy of access: and outside of them waits always this sad portress, Patience; that is to say, the submission to the eternal laws of Pain and Time, and acceptance of them as inevitable, smiling at the grief. So much pains you shall take—so much time you shall wait:—that is the Law. Understand it, honour it; with peace of heart accept the pain, and attend the hours; and as the husbandman in his waiting, you shall see, first the blade, and then the ear, and then the laughing of the valleys. But refuse the Law, and seek to do your work in your own time, or by any serpentine way to evade the pain, and you shall have no harvest—nothing but apples of Sodom: dust shall be your meat, and dust in your throat—there is no singing in such harvest time.

And this is true for all things, little and great. There is a time and a way in which they can be done: none shorter—none smoother. For all noble things, the time is long and the way rude. You may fret and fume as you will; for every start and struggle of impatience there shall be so much attendant failure; if impatience become a habit, nothing but failure: until on the path you have chosen for your better swiftness, rather than the honest flinty one, there shall follow you, fast at hand, instead of Beheste and Art for companions, those two wicked hags,

> " With hoary locks all loose, and visage grim;
> Their feet unshod, their bodies wrapt in rags,
> And both as swift on foot as chased stags;
> And yet the one her other legge had lame,
> Which with a staffe all full of little snags
> She did support, and Impotence her name:
> But th' other was Impatience, armed with raging flame."

" *Raging* flame," note; unserviceable;—flame of the black grain. But the fire which Patience carries in her hand is that truly stolen from Heaven, in the *pith* of the rod—fire of the slow match; persistent Fire like it also in her own body,—fire in the marrow; unquenchable incense of life: though it may seem to the bystanders that there is no breath in her, and she holds herself like a statue, as Hermione, " the statue lady," or Griselda, " the stone lady; " unless indeed one looks close for the glance *forward*, in the eyes, which distinguishes such pillars from the pillars, not of flesh, but of salt, whose eyes are set backwards.

I cannot get to my work in this paper, somehow; the web of these old enigmas entangles me again and again. That rough syllable which begins the name of Griselda, " Gries," " the stone; " the roar of the long fall of the Toccia seems to mix with the sound of it, bringing thoughts of the great Alpine patience; mute snow wreathed by grey rock, till avalanche time comes —patience of mute tormented races till the time of the Grey league came; at last impatient. (Not that, hitherto, it has hewn its way to much: the Rhine-foam of the Via Mala seeming to have done its work better.) But it is a noble colour that Grison Grey;— dawn colour—graceful for a faded silk to ride in, and wonderful, in paper, for getting a g'ow upon, if you begin wisely, as you may some day perhaps see by those Turner sketches at Kensington, if ever anybody can see them.

But we *will* get to work now; the work being to understand, if we may, what tender creatures are indeed riding with us, the British public, in faded silk, and handing our plates for us with tender little thumbs, and never wearing, or doing, anything else (not always having much to put on their own plates). The loveliest arts, the arts of noblest descent, have been long doing this for us, and are still, and we have no idea of their being Princesses, but keep them ill-entreated and enslaved: vociferous as we are against Black slavery, while we are gladly acceptant of Grey; and fain to keep Aglaia and her sisters—Urania and hers,—serving us in faded silk, and taken for kitchen-wenches. We are mad Sanchos, not mad Quixotes; our eyes enchant *Down*wards.

For one instance only: has the reader ever reflected on the patience, and deliberate subtlety, and unostentatious will, involved in the ordinary process of steel engraving; that process of which engravers themselves now with doleful voices deplore the decline, and with sorrowful hearts expect the extinction, after their own days?

By the way—my friends of the field of steel,—you need fear nothing of the kind. What there is of mechanical in your work; of habitual and thoughtless, of vulgar or servile—for that, indeed, the time has come; the sun will burn it up for you, very ruthlessly; but what there is of human liberty, and of sanguine life, in finger and fancy, is kindred of the sun, and quite inextinguishable by him. He is the very last of divinities who would wish to extinguish it. With his red right hand, though full of lightning coruscation, he will faithfully and tenderly clasp yours, warm blooded; you will see the vermilion in the flesh-shadows all the clearer; but your hand will not be withered. I tell you—(dogmatically, if you like to call it so, knowing it well)—a square inch of man's engraving is worth all the photographs that ever were dipped in acid (or left half-washed afterwards, which is saying much) — only it must be man's engraving; not machine's engraving. You have founded a school on patience and labour—only; that school must soon be extinct. You will have to found one on thought, which is Phœnician in immortality, and fears no fire. Believe me, photography can do against line engraving just what Madame Tussaud's wax-work can do against sculpture. That, and no more. You are too timid in this matter; you are like Isaac in that picture of Mr. Schnorr's in the last number of this Journal, and, with Teutonically metaphysical precaution, shade your eyes from the sun with your back to it. Take courage; turn your eyes to it in an aquiline manner; put more sunshine on your steel, and less burr; and leave the photographers to their Phœbus of Magnesium wire.

Not that I mean to speak disrespectfully of magnesium. I honour it to its utmost fiery particle (though I think the soul a fierier one); and I wish the said magnesium all comfort and triumph; nightly-lodging in light-houses, and utter victory over coal gas. Could Titian but have known what the gnomes who built his dolomite crags above Cadore had mixed in the make of them,—and that one day—one night, I mean—his blue distances would still be seen pure blue, by light got out of his own mountains!

Light out of limestone—colour out of coal—and white wings out of hot water! It is a great age this of ours, for traction and extraction, if it only knew what to extract from itself, or where to drag itself to!

But in the meantime I want the public to admire this patience of yours, while they have it, and to understand what it has cost to give them even this, which has to pass away. We will not take instance in figure engraving, of which the complex skill and textural gradation by dot and chequer must be wholly incomprehensible to amateurs; but we will take a piece of

average landscape engraving, such as is sent out of
any good workshop—the master who puts his name
at the bottom of the plate being of course responsible
only for the general method, for the sufficient skill of
subordinate hands, and for the few finishing touches
if necessary. We will take, for example, the plate
of Turner's "Mercury and Argus," engraved in this
Journal.

I suppose most people, looking at such a plate,
fancy it is produced by some simple mechanical artifice,
which is to drawing only what printing is to writing.
They conclude, at all events, that there is something
complacent, sympathetic, and helpful in the nature of
steel; so that while a pen-and-ink sketch may always
be considered an achievement proving cleverness in the
sketcher, a sketch on steel comes out by mere favour
of the indulgent metal: or perhaps they think the plate
is woven like a piece of pattern silk, and the pattern
is developed by pasteboard cards punched full of holes.
Not so. Look close at that engraving—imagine it to
be a drawing in pen and ink, and yourself required
similarly to produce its parallel! True, the steel point
has the one advantage of not blotting, but it has tenfold
or twentyfold disadvantage, in that you cannot slur,
nor efface, except in a very resolute and laborious way,
nor play with it, nor even see what you are doing with
it at the moment, far less the effect that is to be. You
must *feel* what you are doing with it, and know precisely what you have got to do; how deep—how broad
—how far apart—your lines must be, etc. and etc.
(a couple of lines of etc.s would not be enough to imply
all you must know). But suppose the plate *were* only
a pen drawing. Take your pen—your finest—and just
try to copy the leaves that entangle the nearest cow's
head and the head itself; remembering always that the
kind of work required here is mere child's play compared
to that of fine figure engraving. Nevertheless, take a
strong magnifying glass to this—count the dots and

lines that gradate the nostrils and the edges of the
facial bone; notice how the light is left on the top of
the head by the stopping at its outline of the coarse
touches which form the shadows under the leaves;
examine it well, and then—I humbly ask of you—try
to do a piece of it yourself! You clever sketcher—you
young lady or gentleman of genius—you eye-glassed
dilettante—you current writer of criticism royally
plural,—I beseech you—do it yourself; do the merely
etched outline yourself, if no more. Look you,—you
hold your etching needle this way, as you would a
pencil, nearly; and then,—you scratch with it! It is
as easy as lying. Or if you think that too difficult,
take an easier piece;—take either of the light sprays of
foliage that rise against the fortress on the right, put
your glass over them;—look how their fine outline is
first drawn, leaf by leaf; then how the distant rock
is put in between, with broken lines, mostly stopping
before they touch the leaf-outline, and—again, I pray
you, do it yourself; if not on that scale, on a larger.
Go on into the hollows of the distant rock—traverse its
thickets—number its towers—count how many lines
there are in a laurel bush—in an arch—in a casement:
some hundred and fifty, or two hundred, deliberately
drawn lines, you will find, in every square quarter of
an inch; say three thousand to the inch, each with
skilful intent put in its place! and then consider what
the ordinary sketcher's work must appear to the men
who have been trained to this!

"But might not more have been done by three
thousand lines to a square inch?" you will perhaps
ask. Well, possibly. It may be with lines as with
soldiers: three hundred, knowing their work thoroughly,
may be stronger than three thousand less sure of their
game. We shall have to press close home this question
about numbers and purpose presently;—it is not the
question now. Supposing certain results required,—
atmospheric effects, surface textures, transparencies

of shade, confusions of light,—more could *not* be done
with less.   There are engravings of this modern school,
of which, with respect to their particular aim, it may
be said, most truly, they "*cannot* be better done."
Whether an engraving should aim at effects of atmosphere, may be disputable (just as also whether a
sculptor should aim at effects of perspective); but I
do not raise these points to-day.   Admit the aim—
let us note the patience; nor this in engraving only.
I have taken an engraving for my instance, but I might
have taken any form of Art.   I call upon all good
artists, painters, sculptors, metal-workers, to bear
witness with me in what I now tell the public in their
name,—that the same Fortitude, the same deliberation, the same perseverance in resolute act—is needed
to do *anything* in Art that is worthy.   And why is it,
you workmen, that you are silent always concerning
your toil; and mock at us in your hearts, within that
shrine at Eleusis, to the gate of which you have hewn
your way through so deadly thickets of thorn; and
leave us, foolish children, outside, in our conceited
thinking either that we can enter it in play, or that we
are grander for not entering?   Far more earnestly is
it to be asked, why do you *stoop* to us as you mock us?
If your secrecy were a noble one—if, in that incom-
municant contempt, you wrought your own work with
majesty, whether we would receive it or not, it were
kindly, though ungraciously, done; but now you
make yourselves our toys, and do our childish will in
servile silence.   If engraving were to come to an end
this day, and no guided point should press metal more,
do you think it would be in a blaze of glory that your
art would expire?—that those plates in the annuals,
and black proofs in broad shop windows, are of a nobly
monumental character,—" chalybe perennius? "   I am
afraid your patience has been too much like yonder
poor Italian child's; and over that genius of yours,
low laid by the Matin shore, if it expired so, the lament

for Archytas would have to be sung again—"'pulveris exigui—munera." Suppose you were to shake off the dust again! cleanse your wings, like the morning bees on that Matin promontory; rise, in noble *im*patience, for there is such a thing: the Impatience of the Fourth Cornice.

" Cui buon voler, e giusto amor cavalca."

Shall we try, together, to think over the meaning of that Haste, when the May mornings come?

CHAPTER IV

It is a wild March day,—the 20th; and very probably,
due course of English Spring will bring as wild a May-
day by the time this writing meets any one's eyes; but
at all events, as yet the days are rough, and as I look
out of my fitfully lighted window into the garden,
everything seems in a singular hurry. The dead
leaves; and yonder two living ones, on the same stalk,
tumbling over and over each other on the lawn, like a
quaint mechanical toy; and the fallen sticks from the
rooks' nests, and the twisted straws out of the stable-
yard—all going one way, in the hastiest manner!
The puffs of steam, moreover, which pass under the
wooded hills where what used to be my sweetest field-
walk ends now, prematurely, in an abyss of blue clay;
and which signify, in their silvery expiring between the
successive trunks of wintry trees, that some human
beings, thereabouts, are in a hurry as well as the sticks
and straws, and, having fastened themselves to the
tail of a manageable breeze, are being blown down to
Folkstone.

In the general effect of these various passages and
passengers, as seen from my quiet room, they look all
very much alike. One begins seriously to question
with oneself whether those passengers by the Folkstone train are in truth one whit more in a hurry than
the dead leaves. The difference consists, of course, in
the said passengers knowing where they are going to,
and why; and having resolved to go there,—which,
indeed, as far as Folkstone, may, perhaps, properly
distinguish them from the leaves: but will it distinguish them any farther? Do many of them know

what they are going to Folkstone for?—what they are
going anywhere for? and where, at last, by sum of all
the days' journeys, of which this glittering transit is
one, they are going for peace? For if they know not
this, certainly they are no more making haste than
the straws are. Perhaps swiftly going the wrong way;
more likely going no way—any way, as the winds and
their own wills, wilder than the winds, dictate; to find
themselves at last at the end which would have come
to them quickly enough without their seeking.

And, indeed, this is a very preliminary question to
all measurement of the rate of going, this " where to? "
or, even before that, " are we going on at all? "—
" getting on " (as the world says) on any road whatever?
Most men's eyes are so fixed on the mere swirl of the
wheel of their fortunes, and their souls so vexed at the
reversed cadences of it, when they come, that they
forget to ask if the curve they have been carried through
on its circumference was circular or cycloidal; whether
they have been bound to the ups and downs of a mill-
wheel, or of a chariot-wheel.

That phrase, of " getting on," so perpetually on our
lips (as indeed it should be), do any of us take it to our
hearts, and seriously ask where we can get on *to*?
That instinct of hurry has surely good grounds. It is
all very well for lazy and nervous people (like myself
for instance) to retreat into tubs, and holes, and
corners, anywhere out of the dust, and wonder within
ourselves, " what all the fuss can be about? " The
fussy people might have the best of it, if they know
their end. Suppose they were to answer this March
or May morning thus:—" Not bestir ourselves, indeed!
and the spring sun up these four hours!—and this first
of May, 1865, never to come back again; and of Firsts
of May in perspective, supposing ourselves to be 'nel
mezzo del cammin,' perhaps some twenty or twenty-
five to be, not without presumption, hoped for, and
by no means calculated upon. Say, twenty of them,

with their following groups of summer days; and
though they may be long, one cannot make much more
than sixteen hours apiece out of them, poor sleepy
wretches that we are; for even if we get up at four,
we must go to bed while the red yet stays from the
sunset: and half the time we are awake, we must be
lying among haycocks, or playing at something, if we
are wise; not to speak of eating, and previously earning
whereof to eat, which takes time; and then, how much
of us and of our day will be left for getting on? Shall
we have a seventh, or even a tithe, of our twenty-four
hours?—two hours and twenty-four minutes clear, a
day, or, roughly, a thousand hours a year, and (viol-
ently presuming on fortune, as we said) twenty years
of working life: twenty thousand hours to get on in,
altogether? Many men would think it hard to be
limited to an utmost twenty thousand pounds for their
fortunes, but here is a sterner limitation; the Pactolus
of time, sand, and gold together, would, with such a
fortune, count us a pound an hour, through our real
and serviceable life. If this time capital would repro-
duce itself! and for our twenty thousand hours we
could get some rate of interest, if well spent? At all
events, we will do something with them; not lie moping
out of the way of the dust, as you do."

A sufficient answer, indeed; yet, friends, if you
would *make* a little less dust, perhaps we should all see
our way better. But I am ready to take the road with
you, if you mean it so seriously—only let us at least
consider where we are now, at starting.

Here, on a little spinning, askew-axised thing we
call a planet—(impertinently enough, since we are far
more planetary ourselves). A round, rusty, rough
little metallic ball—very hard to live upon; most of it
much too hot or too cold: a couple of narrow habitable
belts about it, which, to wandering spirits, must look
like the places where it has got damp, and green-mouldy,
with accompanying small activities of animal life in

the midst of the lichen.   Explosive gases, seemingly, inside it, and possibilities of very sudden dispersion.

This is where we are; and round about us, there seem to be more of such balls, variously heated and chilled, ringed and mooned, moved, and comforted; the whole giddy group of us forming an atom in a milky mist, itself another atom in a shoreless phosphorescent sea of such Volvoces and Medusae.

Whereupon, I presume, one would first ask, have we any chance of getting off this ball of ours, and getting on to one of those finer ones?   Wise people say we have, and that it is very wicked to think otherwise. So we will think no otherwise; but, with their permission, think nothing about the matter now, since it is certain that the more we make of our little rusty world, such as it is, the more chance we have of being one day promoted into a merrier one.

And even on this rusty and mouldy Earth, there appear to be things which may be seen with pleasure, and things which might be done with advantage.   The stones of it have strange shapes; the plants and the beasts of it strange ways.   Its air is coinable into wonderful sounds; its light into manifold colours: the trees of it bring forth pippins, and the fields cheese (though both of these may be, in a finer sense, " to come ").   There are bright eyes upon it which reflect the light of other eyes quite singularly; and foolish feelings to be cherished upon it; and gladdenings of dust by neighbour dust, not easily explained, but pleasant, and which take time to win.   One would like to know something of all this, I suppose?—to divide one's score of thousand hours as shrewdly as might be. Ten minutes to every herb of the field is not much; yet we shall not know them all, so, before the time comes to be made grass of ourselves!   Half an hour for every crystalline form of clay and flint, and we shall be near the need of shaping the grey flint stone that is to weigh upon our feet.   And we would fain dance a

measure or two before that cumber is laid upon them:
there having been hitherto much piping to which we
have not danced.   And we must leave time for loving,
if we are to take Marmontel's wise peasant's word for
it, " *Il n'y a de bon que c'a !* "   And if there should be
fighting to do also? and sweeping ? and much bury-
ing? truly, we had better make haste.

Which means, simply, that we must lose neither
strength nor moment.   Hurry is not haste; but
economy is, and rightness is.   Whatever is rightly done
stays with us, to support another right beyond, or
higher up: whatever is wrongly done, vanishes; and
by the blank, betrays what we would have built above.
Wasting no word, no thought, no doing, we shall have
speed enough; but then there is that farther question,
what shall we do?—what we are fittest (worthiest, that
is) to do, and what is best worth doing?   Note that
word, " worthy," both of the man and the thing, for
the two dignities go together.   Is *it* worth the pains?
Are we worth the task?   The dignity of a man depends
wholly upon this harmony.   If his task is above him,
he will be undignified in failure; if he is above it, he
will be undigned in success.   His own composure and
nobleness must be according to the composure of his
thought to his toil.

As I was dreaming over this, my eyes fell by chance
on a page of my favourite thirteenth-century psalter,
just where two dragons, one with red legs, and another
with green,—one with a blue tail on a purple ground,
and the other with a rosy tail on a golden ground,
follow the verse, " *Quis ascendet in montem Domini,*"
and begin the solemn " *Qui non accepit in vano animam
suam.*"   Who hath not lift up his soul unto vanity, we
have it ; and ἔλαβεν ἐπὶ ματαίῳ, the Greeks (not
that I know what that means accurately): broadly,
they all mean, " who has not received nor given his
soul in vain," this is the man who can make haste, even
up hill, the only haste worth making; and it must be up

L

the right hill, too: not that Corinthian Acropolis, of which, I suppose, the white spectre stood eighteen hundred feet high, in Hades, for Sisyphus to roll his fantastic stone up—image, himself, for ever of the greater part of our wise mortal work.

Now all this time, whatever the reader may think, I have never for a moment lost sight of that original black line with which is our own special business. The patience, the speed, the dignity, we can give to that, the choice to be made of subject for it, are the matters I want to get at. You think, perhaps, that an engraver's function is one of no very high dignity;—does not involve a serious choice of work. Consider a little of it. Here is a steel point, and 'tis like Job's " iron pen "— and you are going to cut into steel with it, in a most deliberate way, as into the rock for ever. And this scratch or inscription of yours will be seen of a multitude of eyes. It is not like a single picture or a single wall painting; this multipliable work will pass through thousand thousand hands, strengthen and inform innumerable souls, if it be worthy, vivify the folly of thousands if unworthy. Remember, also, it will mix in the very closest manner in domestic life. This engraving will not be gossiped over and fluttered past at private views of academies; listlessly sauntered by in corners of great galleries. Ah, no! This will hang over parlour chimney-pieces—shed down its hourly influence on children's forenoon work. This will hang in little luminous corners by sick beds; mix with flickering dreams by candlelight, and catch the first rays from the window's " glimmering square." You had better put something good into it! I do not know a more solemn field of labour than that *champ d'acier*. From a pulpit, perhaps a man can only reach one or two people, for that time,—even your book, once carelessly read, probably goes into a book-case catacomb, and is thought of no more. But this; taking the eye unawares again and again, and always again: persisting and inevitable!

where will you look for a chance of saying something
nobly, if it is not here?

And the choice is peculiarly free; to you of all men
most free. An artist, at first invention, cannot always
choose what shall come into his mind, nor know what
it will eventually turn into. But you, professed copyists,
unless you have mistaken your profession, have the
power of governing your own thoughts and of following
and interpreting the thoughts of others. Also, you see
the work to be done put plainly before you; you can
deliberately choose what seems to you best, out of
myriads of examples of perfect Art. You can count
the cost accurately; saying, " It will take me a year—
two years—five—a fourth or fifth, probably, of my
remaining life, to do this." Is the thing worth it?
There is no excuse for choosing wrongly; no other men
whatever have data so full, and position so firm, for
forecast of their labour.

I put my psalter aside (not, observe, vouching for its
red and green dragons:—men lifted up their souls to
vanity sometimes in the thirteenth as in the nineteenth
century), and I take up, instead, a book of English
verses, published—there is no occasion to say when.
It is full of costliest engravings—large, skilful, appal-
lingly laborious; dotted into textures like the dust on a
lily leaf,—smoothed through gradations like clouds,—
graved to surfaces like mother-of-pearl; and by all this
toil there is set forth for the delight of English women,
a series of the basest dreams that ungoverned feminine
imagination can coin in sickliest indolence,—ball-room
amours, combats of curled knights, pilgrimages of disguised girl-pages, romantic pieties, charities in costume,
—a mass of disguised sensualism and feverish vanity—
impotent, pestilent, prurient, scented with a venomous
elixir, and rouged with a deadly dust of outward good;
and all this done, as such things only can be done, in a
boundless ignorance of all natural veracity; the faces
falsely drawn—the lights falsely cast—the forms effaced

or distorted, and all common human wit and sense
extinguished in the vicious scum of lying sensation.

And this, I grieve to say, is only a characteristic
type of a large mass of popular English work. This is
what we spend our Teutonic lives, in engraving with an
iron pen in the rock for ever; this, the passion of the
Teutonic woman (as opposed to Virgilia), just as fox-
hunting is the passion of the Teutonic man, as opposed
to Valerius.

And while we deliberately spend all our strength, and
all our tenderness, all our skill, and all our money, in
doing, relishing, buying, this absolute Wrongness, of
which nothing can ever come but disease in heart and
brain, remember that all the mighty works of the great
painters of the world, full of life, truth, and blessing,
remain to this present hour of the year 1865 unen-
graved. There literally exists no earnestly studied and
fully accomplished engraving of any very great work,
except Leonardo's Cena. No large Venetian picture
has ever been thoroughly engraved. Of Titian's Peter
Martyr, there is even no worthy memorial transcript
but Le Febre's. The Cartoons have been multiplied
in false readings; never in faithful ones till lately by
photography. Of the Disputa and the Parnassus,
what can the English public know? of the thoughtful
Florentines and Milanese, of Ghirlandajo, and Luini,
and their accompanying hosts—what do they yet so
much as care to know?

" The English public will not pay," you reply, " for
engravings from the great masters. The English public
will only pay for pictures of itself; of its races, its rifle-
meetings, its rail stations, its parlour-passions, and
kitchen interests; you must make your bread as you
may, by holding the mirror to it."

Friends, there have been hard fighting and heavy
sleeping, this many a day, on the other side of the
Atlantic, in the cause, as you suppose, of Freedom
against slavery; and you are all, open-mouthed, ex-

pecting the glories of Black Emancipation. Perhaps
a little White Emancipation on this side of the water
might be still more desirable, and more easily and
guiltlessly won.

Do you know what slavery means? Suppose a
gentleman taken by a Barbary corsair—set to field-
work; chained and flogged to it from dawn to eve.
Need he be a slave therefore? By no means; he is but
a hardly-treated prisoner. There is some work which
the Barbary corsair will not be able to make him do;
such work as a Christian gentleman may not do,
that he will not, though he die for it. Bound and
scourged he may be, but he has heard of a Person's
being bound and scourged before now, who was not
therefore a slave. He is not a whit more slave for that.
But suppose he take the pirate's pay, and stretch his
back at piratical oars, for due salary, how then? Suppose for fitting price he betray his fellow prisoners, and
take up the scourge instead of enduring it—become the
smiter instead of the smitten, at the African's bidding—
how then? Of all the sheepish notions in our English
public " mind," I think the simplest is that slavery is
neutralised when you are well paid for it! Whereas it
is precisely that fact of its being paid for which makes
it complete. A man who has been sold by another,
may be but half a slave or none; but the man who has
sold himself! He is the accurately Finished Bondsman.

And gravely I say that I know *no* captivity so sorrowful as that of an artist doing, consciously, bad work for
pay. It is the serfdom of the finest gifts—of all that
should lead and master men, offering itself to be spit
upon, and that for a bribe. There is much serfdom,
in Europe, of speakers and writers, but they only sell
words; and their talk, even honestly uttered, might not
have been worth much; it will not be thought of ten
years hence; still less a hundred years hence. No one
will buy our parliamentary speeches to keep in port-
folios this time next century; and if people are weak

enough now to pay for any special and flattering cadence of syllable, it is little matter. But *you*, with your painfully acquired power, your unwearied patience, your admirable and manifold gifts, your eloquence in black and white, which people will buy, if it is good (and has a broad margin), for fifty guineas a copy—in the year 2000; to sell it all, as Ananias his land, " yea, for so much," and hold yourselves at every fool's beck, with your ready points, polished and sharp, hasting to scratch what *he* wills! To bite permanent mischief in with acid; to spread an inked infection of evil all your days, and pass away at last from a life of the skilfullest industry—having done whatsoever your hand found (remuneratively) to do, with your might, and a great might, but with cause to thank God only for this—that the end of it all has at last come, and that " there is no device nor work in the Grave." One would get quit of *this* servitude, I think, though we reached the place of Rest a little sooner, and reached it fasting.

My English fellow-workmen, you have the name of liberty often on your lips; get the fact of it oftener into your business; talk of it less, and try to understand it better. You have given students many copy-books of free-hand outlines—give them a few of free *heart* outlines.

It appears, however, that you do not intend to help me with any utterance respecting these same outlines.[1] Be it so: I must make out what I can by myself. And under the influence of the Solstitial sign of June I will go backwards, or askance, to the practical part of the business, where I left it, three months ago, and take up that question first, touching Liberty, and the relation

---

[1] I have received some interesting private letters, but cannot make use of them at present, because they enter into general discussion instead of answering the specific question I asked, respecting the power of the black line; and I must observe to correspondents that in future their letters should be addressed to the Editor of this Journal, not to me; as I do not wish to incur the responsibility of selection.

of the loose swift line to the resolute slow one, and of the etched line to the engraved one. It is a worthy question, for the open field afforded by illustrated works is tempting even to our best painters, and many an earnest hour and active fancy spend and speak themselves in the black line, vigorously enough, and dramatically, at all events: if wisely, may be considered. The French also are throwing great passion into their *eaux fortes*—working with a vivid haste and dark, brilliant freedom, which looks as if they etched with very energetic waters indeed—quite waters of life (it does not look so well, written in French). So we will take, with the reader's permission, for text next month, " Rembrandt, and strong waters."

CHAPTER V

THE work I have to do in this paper ought, rightly, to have been thrown into the form of an appendix to the last chapter; for it is no link of the cestus of Aglaia we have to examine, but one of the crests of canine passion in the cestus of Scylla. Nevertheless, the girdle of the Grace cannot be discerned in the full brightness of it, but by comparing it with the dark torment of that other; and (in what place or form matters little) the work has to be done.

"Rembrandt Van Rhyn"—it is said, in the last edition of a very valuable work [1] (for which, nevertheless, I could wish that greater lightness in the hand should be obtained by the publication of its information in one volume, and its criticism in another)—was "the most attractive and original of painters." It may be so; but there are attractions, and attractions. The sun attracts the planets—and a candle, night-moths; the one with perhaps somewhat of benefit to the planets;—but with what benefit the other to the moths, one would be glad to learn from those desert flies, of whom, one company having extinguished Mr. Kinglake's candle with their bodies, the remainder, "who had failed in obtaining this martyrdom, became suddenly serious, and clung despondingly to the canvas."

Also, there are originalities, and originalities. To invent a new thing, which is also a precious thing; to

[1] Wornum's *Epochs of Painting.* I have continual occasion to quarrel with my friend on these matters of critical question; but I have deep respect for his earnest and patient research, and we remain friends—on the condition that I am to learn much from him, and he (though it may be questionable whose fault that is) nothing from me.

be struck by a divinely-guided Rod, and become a sudden fountain of life to thirsty multitudes—this is enviable. But to be distinct of men in an original Sin, elect for the initial letter of a Lie; the first apparent spot of an unknown plague; a Root of bitterness, and the first-born worm of a company, studying an original De-Composition,—this is perhaps not so enviable. And if we think of it, most human originality is apt to be of that kind. Goodness is one, and immortal; it may be received and communicated—not originated: but Evil is various and recurrent, and may be misbegotten in endlessly surprising ways.

But, that we may know better in what this originality consists, we find that our author, after expatiating on the vast area of the Pantheon, " illuminated solely by the small circular opening in the dome above," and on other similar conditions of luminous contraction, tells us that " to Rembrandt belongs the glory of having first embodied in Art, and perpetuated, these rare and beautiful effects of nature." Such effects are indeed rare in nature; but they are not rare, absolutely. The sky, with the sun in it, does not usually give the impression of being dimly lighted through a circular hole; but you may observe a very similar effect any day in your coal-cellar. The light is not Rembrandtesque on the current, or banks, of a river; but it is on those of a drain. Colour is not Rembrandtesque, usually, in a clean house; but is presently obtainable of that quality in a dirty one. And without denying the pleasantness of the mode of progression which Mr. Hazlitt, perhaps too enthusiastically, describes as attainable in a background of Rembrandt's—" You stagger from one abyss of obscurity to another "—I cannot feel it an entirely glorious speciality to be distinguished, as Rembrandt was, from other great painters, chiefly by the liveliness of his darkness, and the dullness of his light. Glorious, or inglorious, the speciality itself is easily and accurately definable. It is the aim of the best painters to paint

the noblest things they can see by sunlight.   It was the
aim of Rembrandt to paint the foulest things he could
see—by rushlight.

By rushlight, observe: material and spiritual.   As
the sun for the outer world; so in the inner world of
man, that which " ἐρευνᾷ ταμιεῖα κοιλίας " [1] — " the
candle of God, searching the inmost parts."   If that
light within become but a more active kind of darkness;
—if, abdicating the measuring reed of modesty for
sceptre, and ceasing to measure with it, we dip it in
such unctuous and inflammable refuse as we can find,
and make our soul's light into a *tallow* candle, and
thenceforward take our guttering, sputtering, ill-smell-
ing illumination about with us, holding it out in fetid
fingers—encumbered with its lurid warmth of fungous
wick, and drip of stalactitic grease—that we may see,
when another man would have seen, or dreamed he saw,
the flight of a divine Virgin—only the lamp-light upon
the hair of a costermonger's ass;—that, having to
paint the good Samaritan, we may see only in distance
the back of the good Samaritan, and in nearness the
back of the good Samaritan's dog;—that having to
paint the Annunciation to the Shepherds, we may turn
the announcement of peace to men, into an announcement of mere panic to beasts; and, in an unsightly
firework of unsightlier angels, see, as we see always, the
feet instead of the head, and the shame instead of the
honour;—and finally concentrate and rest the sum of
our fame, as Titian on the Assumption of a spirit, so we
on the dissection of a carcase,—perhaps by such fatuous
fire, the less we walk, and by such phosphoric glow, the
less we shine, the better it may be for us, and for all who
would follow us.

Do not think I deny the greatness of Rembrandt.
In mere technical power (none of his eulogists know
that power better than I, nor declare it in more distinct
terms) he might, if he had been educated in a true school,

[1] Prov. xix. 27.

have taken rank with the Venetians themselves. But
that type of distinction between Titian's Assumption,
and Rembrandt's Dissection, will represent for you
with sufficient significance the manner of choice in all
their work; only it should be associated with another
characteristic example of the same opposition (which
I have dwelt upon elsewhere) between Veronese and
Rembrandt, in their conception of domestic life.
Rembrandt's picture, at Dresden, of himself, with his
wife sitting on his knee, a roasted peacock on the table,
and a glass of champagne in his hand, is the best work
I know of all he has left; and it marks his speciality
with entire decision. It is, of course, a dim candlelight; and the choice of the sensual passions as the
things specially and for ever to be described and immor-
talised out of his own private life and love, is exactly
that " painting the foulest thing by rushlight " which
I have stated to be the enduring purpose of his mind.
And you will find this hold in all minor treatment; and
that to the uttermost: for as by your broken rushlight
you see little, and only corners and points of things, and
those very corners and points ill and distortedly; so,
although Rembrandt knows the human face and hand,
and never fails in these, when they are ugly, and he
chooses to take pains with them, he knows nothing else:
the more pains he takes with even familiar animals, the
worse they are (witness the horse in that plate of the
good Samaritan), and any attempts to finish the first
scribbled energy of his imaginary lions and tigers, end
always only in the loss of the fiendish power and rage
which were all he could conceive in an animal.

His landscape, and foreground vegetation, I mean
afterwards to examine in comparison with Durer's;
but the real calibre and nature of the man are best to be
understood by comparing the puny, ill-drawn, terror-
less, helpless, beggarly skeleton in his " Youth Surprised by Death," with the figure behind the trees in
Durer's plate (though it is quite one of Durer's feeblest)

of the same subject. Absolutely ignorant of all natural phenomena and law; absolutely careless of all lovely living form, or growth, or structure; able only to render with some approach to veracity, what alone he had looked at with some approach to attention,—the pawnbroker's festering heaps of old clothes, and caps, and shoes—Rembrandt's execution is one grand evasion, and his temper the grim contempt of a strong and sullen animal in its defiled den, for the humanity with which it is at war, for the flowers which it tramples, and the light which it fears.

Again, do not let it be thought that when I call his execution evasive, I ignore the difference between his touch, on brow or lip, and a common workman's; but the whole school of etching which he founded, (and of painting, so far as it differs from Venetian work) is inherently loose and experimental. Etching is the very refuge and mask of sentimental uncertainty, and of vigorous ignorance. If you know anything clearly, and have a firm hand, depend upon it, you will draw it clearly; you will not care to hide it among scratches and burrs. And herein is the first grand distinction between etching and engraving—that in the etching needle you have an almost irresistible temptation to a wanton speed. There is, however, no real necessity for such a distinction; an etched line may have been just as steadily drawn, and seriously meant, as an engraved one; and for the moment, waiving consideration of this distinction, and opposing Rembrandt's work, considered merely as work of the black line, to Holbein's and Durer's, as work of the black line, I assert Rembrandt's to be inherently *evasive*. You cannot unite his manner with theirs;—choice between them is sternly put to you, when first you touch the steel. Suppose, for instance, you have to engrave, or etch, or draw with pen and ink, a single head, and that the head is to be approximately half an inch in height, more or less (there is a reason for assigning this condition

respecting size, which we will examine in due time): you
have it in your power to do it in one of two ways. You
may lay down some twenty or thirty entirely firm and
visible lines, of which every one shall be absolutely
right, and do the utmost a line can do. By their cur-
vature they shall render contour; by their thickness,
shade; by their place and form, every truth of expression, and every condition of design. The head of the
soldier drawing his sword, in Durer's " Cannon," is
about half an inch high, supposing the brow to be seen.
The chin is drawn with three lines, the lower lip with
two, the upper, including the shadow from the nose,
with five. Three separate the cheek from the chin,
giving the principal points of character. Six lines
draw the cheek, and its incised traces of care; four are
given to each of the eyes; one, with the outline, to the
nose; three to the frown of the forehead. None of
these touches could anywhere be altered—none removed,
without instantly visible harm; and their result is a
head as perfect in character as a portrait by Reynolds.

You may either do this—which, if you can, it will
generally be very advisable to do—or, on the other hand,
you may cover the face with innumerable scratches,
and let your hand play with wanton freedom, until the
graceful scrabble concentrates itself into shade. You
may soften—efface—retouch—rebite—dot, and hatch,
and redefine. If you are a great master, you will soon
get your character, and probably keep it (Rembrandt
often gets it at first, nearly as securely as Durer); but
the design of it will be necessarily seen through loose
work, and modified by accident (as you think) fortunate. The accidents which occur to a practised hand
are always at first pleasing—the details which can be
hinted, however falsely, through the gathering mystery,
are always seducing. You will find yourself gradually
dwelling more and more on little meannesses of form
and texture, and lustres of surface: on cracks of skin,
and films of fur and plume. You will lose your way,

and then see two ways, and then many ways, and try
to walk a little distance on all of them in turn, and so,
back again.   You will find yourself thinking of colours,
and vexed because you cannot imitate them; next,
struggling to render distances by indecision, which you
cannot by tone.   Presently you will be contending with
finished pictures; labouring at the etching, as if it were
a painting.   You will leave off, after a whole day's work
(after many days' work if you choose to give them),
still unsatisfied.   For final result—if you are as great
as Rembrandt—you will have most likely a heavy, black,
cloudy stain, with less character in it than the first ten
lines had.   If you are not as great as Rembrandt, you
will have a stain by no means cloudy; but sandy and
broken,—instead of a face, a speckled phantom of a face,
patched, blotched, discomfited in every texture and
form—ugly, assuredly; dull, probably; an unmanageable and manifold failure ill concealed by momentary,
accidental, undelightful, ignoble success.

Undelightful; note this especially, for it is the
peculiar character of etching that it cannot render
beauty.   You may hatch and scratch your way to
picturesqueness or to deformity—never to beauty.
You can etch an old woman, or an ill-conditioned fellow.
But you cannot etch a girl—nor, unless in his old age,
or with very partial rendering of him, a gentleman.

And thus, as farther belonging to, and partly causa-
tive of, their choice of means, there is always a tendency
in etchers to fasten on unlovely objects; and the whole
scheme of modern rapid work of this kind is connected
with a peculiar gloom which results from the confine-
ment of men, partially informed, and wholly untrained,
in the midst of foul and vicious cities.   A sensitive and
imaginative youth, early driven to get his living by his
art, has to lodge, we will say, somewhere in the by-
streets of Paris, and is left there, tutorless, to his own
devices.   Suppose him also vicious or reckless, and
there need be no talk of his work farther; he will cer-

tainly do nothing in a Dureresque manner. But suppose him self-denying, virtuous, full of gift and power—
what are the elements of living study within his reach?
All supreme beauty is confined to the higher salons.
There are pretty faces in the streets, but no stateliness
nor splendour of humanity; all pathos and grandeur is
in suffering; no purity of nature is accessible, but only
a terrible picturesqueness, mixed with ghastly, with
ludicrous, with base concomitants. Huge walls and
roofs, dark on the sunset sky, but plastered with advertisement bills, monstrous-figured, seen farther than ever
Parthenon shaft, or spire of Sainte Chapelle. Inter-
minable lines of massy streets, wearisome with repetition of commonest design, and degraded by their gilded
shops, wide-fuming, flaunting, glittering, with apparatus
of eating or of dress. Splendour of palace-flank and
goodly quay, insulted by floating cumber of barge and
bath, trivial, grotesque, indecent, as cleansing vessels in
a royal reception room. Solemn avenues of blossomed
trees, shading puppet-show and baby-play; glades of
wild-wood, long withdrawn, purple with faded shadows
of blood; sweet windings and reaches of river far among
the brown vines and white orchards, checked here by
the Ile Notre Dame, to receive their nightly sacrifice,
and after playing with it among their eddies, to give it
up again, in those quiet shapes that lie on the sloped
slate tables of the square-built Temple of the Death-
Sibyl, who presides here over spray of Seine, as yonder
at Tibur over spray of Anio. Sibylline, indeed, in her
secrecy, and her sealing of destinies, by the baptism of
the quick water-drops which fall on each fading face,
unrecognised, nameless in *this* Baptism for ever.
Wreathed thus throughout, that Paris town, with
beauty, and with unseemly sin, unseemlier death, as a
fiend-city with fair eyes; for ever letting fall her silken
raiment so far as that one may " behold her bosom and
half her side." Under whose whispered teaching and
substitution of " Contes Drolatiques " for the tales of the

wood fairy, her children of Imagination will do, what
Jérome and Gustave Doré are doing, and her whole
world of lesser Art will sink into shadows of the street
and of the boudoir-curtain, wherein the etching point
may disport itself with freedom enough.[1]

Nor are we slack in our companionship in these
courses. Our imagination is slower and clumsier than

[1] As I was preparing these sheets for press, I chanced on a
passage in a novel of Champfleury's, in which one young student
is encouraging another in his contest with these and other such
evils;—the evils are in this passage accepted as necessities; the
inevitable deadliness of the element is not seen, as it can hardly
be except by those who live out of it. The encouragement, on
such view, is good and right; the connection of the young etcher's
power with his poverty is curiously illustrative of the statements
in the text, and the whole passage, though long, is well worth
such space as it will ask here, in our small print.

" Cependant," dit Thomas, " on a vu des peintres de talent
qui étaient partis de Paris après avoir exposé de bons tableaux et
qui s'en revenaient classiquement ennuyeux. C'est donc la
faute de l'enseignement de l'Académie."

" Bah! " dit Gérard, " rien n'errête le développement d'un
homme de talent: ni la mis re, ni la maladie, ni les faux conseils,
ni les mauvais enseignements. Nous sommes environnés d'ennuyeux, d'imbéciles, de traîtres, de lâches; si nous sommes forts,
nous devons nous débarrasser de tous ces ennemis. Si nous
n'avons pas le courage, c'est-à-dire une conviction profonde de
l'art, nous succumbons, tant pis, il n'y a rien à dire. Nous ne
sommes pas des victimes, nous n'étions pas dignes de faire de
l'art, et nous sommes entrés pas erreur dans ce beau et rude
chemin qui mène à la popularité. On est doué, ou on ne l'est
pas."

.   .   .   .

" Pourtant j'ai connu plus d'un peintre que la misère a paralysé
complétement, et qui, avec un peu d'aide, eût produit de belles
choses. Au lieu de cela, il est tombé dans les mains des mar-
chands, et il s'est livré à de honteuses lithographies."

" C'est qu'il était né pour faire de pareilles lithographies."

" Mais," dit Thomas, " il pleure d'être obligé de faire du commerce."

" Il fait semblant de pleurer."

" Non, non," dit Thomas.

" Alors il se trompe sur lui-même: puisqu'il comprend l'art,
pourquoi ne fait-il pas d'art? "

" Parce qu'il gagne à peu près sa vie en faisant du commerce."

" On dirait que tu ne veux pas me comprendre, toi qui as juste-
ment passé par là. Comment faisais-tu quand tu étais com-
positeur d'une imprimerie? "

" Le soir," dit Thomas, " et le matin en hiver, à partir de

the French—rarer also, by far, in the average English
mind.   The only man of power equal to Doré's whom
we have had lately among us, was William Blake, whose
temper fortunately took another turn.   But in the
calamity and vulgarity of daily circumstance, in the
horror of our streets, in the discordance of our thoughts,
in the laborious looseness and ostentatious cleverness
of our work, we are alike.   And to French faults we add
a stupidity of our own; for which, so far as I may in
modesty take blame for anything, as resulting from my

quatre heures, je faisais des études à la lampe pendant deux
heures, jusqu'au moment où j'allais à l'atelier."
" Et tu ne vivais pas de la peinture? "
" Je ne gagnais pas un sou."
" Bon! " dit Gérard; " tu vois bien que tu faisais du commerce
en dehors de l'art et que cependant tu étudiais.   Quand tu es
sorti de l'imprimerie, comment as-tu vécu? "
" Je faisais cinq ou six petites aquarelles par jour, que je
vendais, sous les arcades de l'Institut, six sous pièce."
" Et tu en vivais; c'est encore du commerce.   Tu vois donc
que ni l'imprimerie, ni les petits dessins, à cinq sous, ni la priva-
tion, ni la misère ne t'ont empêché d'arriver."
" Je ne suis pas arrivé."
" N'importe, tu arriveras certainement. . . . Si tu veux
d'autres exemples qui prouvent que la misère et les autres piéges
tendus sous nos pas ne doivent rien arrêter, tu te rappelles bien
ce pauvre garçon dont vous admiriez les eaux-fortes, que vous
mettiez aussi haut que Rembrandt, et qui aurait été loin, disiez-
vous, s'il n'avait tant souffert de la faim.   Qu'a-t-il fait le jour
où il lui est tombé un petit héritage du ciel? "
" Il est vrai," dit Thomas, embarrassé; " qu'il a perdu tout
son sentiment."
" Ce n'était pas cependant une de ces grosses fortunes qui
tuent un homme, qui le rendent lourd, fier et insolent: il avait
juste de quoi vivre, six cents francs de rentes, une fortune pour
lui, qui vivait avec cinq francs par mois.   Il a continué à tra-
vailler; mais ses eaux-fortes n'étaient plus supportables; tandis
qu'avant, il vivait avec un morceau de pain et des légumes; alors
il avait du talent.   Cela, Thomas, doit te prouver que ni les
mauvais enseignements, ni les influences, ni la misère, ni la faim,
ni la maladie, ne peuvent corrompre une nature bien douée.
Elle souffre; mais trouve moi un grand artiste qui n'ait pas souffert.
Il n'y a pas un seul homme de génie heureux depuis que l'humanité
existe."
" J'ai envie," dit Thomas, " de te faire cadeau d'une jolie
cravate."
" Pourquoi? " dit Gérard.
" Parce que tu as bien parlé."

own teaching, I am more answerable than most men. Having spoken earnestly against painting without thinking, I now find our exhibitions decorated with works of students who think without painting; and our books illustrated by scratched woodcuts, representing very ordinary people, who are presumed to be interesting in the picture, because the text tells a story about them. Of this least lively form of modern sensational work, however, I shall have to speak on other grounds; meantime, I am concerned only with its manner; its incontinence of line and method, associated with the slightness of its real thought, and morbid acuteness of irregular sensation; ungoverned all, and one of the external and slight phases of that beautiful Liberty which we are proclaiming as essence of gospel to all the earth, and shall presently, I suppose, when we have had enough of it here, proclaim also to the stars, with invitation to them *out* of their courses.

" But you asked us for ' free-heart ' outlines, and told us not to be slaves, only thirty days ago."

Inconsistent that I am! so I did. But as there are attractions, and attractions; originalities, and originalities, there are liberties, and liberties. Yonder torrent, crystal-clear, and arrow-swift, with its spray leaping into the air like white troops of fawns, is free, I think. Lost, yonder, amidst bankless, boundless marsh —soaking in slow shallowness, as it will, hither and thither, listless, among the poisonous reeds and unresisting slime—it is free also. You may choose which liberty you will, and the restraint of voiceful rock, or the dumb and edgeless shore of darkened sand. Of that evil liberty, which men are now glorifying, and of its opposite continence—which is the clasp and χρυσέη περόνη of Aglaia's cestus—we will try to find out something in next chapter.

CHAPTER VI

No quality of Art has been more powerful in its influence on public mind;—none is more frequently the
subject of popular praise, or the end of vulgar effort,
than what we call "Freedom." It is necessary to
determine the justice or injustice of this popular praise.

I said, a little while ago, that the practical teaching
of the masters of Art was summed by the **0** of Giotto.
Yet that cypher may become, if rightly read, an expression of infinity, at least in one direction of teaching.
"You may judge my masterhood of craft," Giotto tells
us, "by seeing that I can draw a circle unerringly."
And we may safely believe him, understanding him to
mean that—though more may be necessary to an artist
than such a power—at least *this* power is necessary.
The qualities of hand and eye needful to do this are the
first conditions of artistic craft.

Try to draw a circle yourself with a "free" hand, and
with a single line. You cannot do it if your hand
trembles, nor if it hesitates, nor if it is unmanageable,
nor if it is in the common sense of the word "free."
So far from being free, it must be under a control as
absolute and accurate as if it were fastened to an in-
flexible bar of steel. And yet it must move, under this
necessary control, with perfect, untormented serenity
of ease.

That is the condition of all good work whatsoever.
All freedom is error. Every line you lay down is either
right or wrong: it may be timidly and awkwardly wrong,
or fearlessly and impudently wrong: the aspect of the
impudent wrongness is pleasurable to vulgar persons,
and is what is commonly called "free" execution: the

timid, tottering, hesitating wrongness is rarely so attractive; yet sometimes, if accompanied with good qualities, and right aims in other directions, it becomes in a manner charming, like the inarticulateness of a child: but, whatever the charm or the manner of the error, there is but one question ultimately and seriously to be asked respecting every line you draw, Is it right or wrong? If right, it most assuredly is not a " free " line, but an intensely continent, restrained, and considered line; and the action of the hand in laying it is just as decisive, and just as " free " as the hand of a first-rate surgeon in a critical incision. A great operator told me that his hand could check itself within about the two-hundredth of an inch, in penetrating a membrane; and this, of course, without the help of sight, by sensation only. With help of sight, and in action on a substance which does not quiver nor yield, a fine artist's line is measurable in its purposed direction to considerably less than the thousandth of an inch.

A wide freedom, truly!

The conditions of popular Art which most foster the common ideas about freedom are merely results of irregularly energetic effort by men imperfectly educated; these conditions being variously mingled with cruder mannerisms resulting from timidity, or actual imperfection of body. Northern hands and eyes are, of course, never so subtle as Southern, and in very cold countries artistic execution is in a manner palsied. The effort to break through this rigidity, or to refine the bluntness, leads, in some of the greatest Northern masters, to a licentious sweep and stormy impetuosity of hand; or in the meanest, to an ostentatious and microscopic minuteness. Every man's manner has relation to his physical powers and modes of thought, but in the greatest work there is no manner visible. It is at first uninteresting from its quietness; the majesty of restrained power only dawns gradually upon us, as we walk towards its horizon.

There is often great delightfulness in the innocent manners of artists who have real power and honesty, and draw, in this way or that, as best they can, under such and such untoward circumstances of life. Thus the execution of Prout was that of a master with great and true sentiment for the pathos of ruin, with great and ready power of arrangement of masses, and fine sense of light and shade; but uneducated, and near-sighted. Make a scholar of such an one, and give him good eyes, and it is impossible for him to draw in that way again; how he would have drawn, one cannot say; but it would have been wholly and exaltedly otherwise. The execution of Cox is merely a condition of Northern palsy, through which, in a blundering way, a true sense of certain modes of colour, and of the sweetness of certain natural scenes, finds innocent expression.

So even with the great old William Hunt: whatever was peculiar in his execution, broken, spotty, or clumsy, is the character of a rustic, partly of a physically feeble hand; the exquisite truth which is seen by the subtle mind gives a charm to the expression, as to a country dialect. But the looseness and flimsiness of modern etching and wood engraving are very different from these manners, and far less pardonable; being more or less affected, and in great part the expression of an inner spirit of licence in mind and heart, connected, as I said, with the peculiar folly of this age, its hope of, and trust in, " Liberty." Of which we must reason a little in more general terms.

I believe we can nowhere find a better type of a perfectly free creature than in the common house-fly. Nor free only, but brave; and irreverent to a degree which I think no human republican could by any philosophy raise himself to. There is no courtesy in him; he does not care whether it is king or clown whom he teases; and in every step of his swift mechanical march, and in every pause of his resolute observation, there is one and the same expression of perfect egotism, perfect

independence and self-confidence, and conviction of the
world's having been made for flies.   Strike at him with
your hand.   To him the mechanical fact and external
aspect of the matter is, what to you it would be, if an
acre of red clay, ten feet thick, tore itself up from the
ground in one massive field, hovered over you in the air
for a second, and came crashing down with an aim!
That is the external aspect of it; the inner aspect, to his
fly's mind, is of a quite natural and unimportant occurrence—one of the momentary conditions of his active
life.   He steps out of the way of your hand, and alights
on the back of it.   You cannot terrify him, nor govern
him, nor persuade him, nor convince him.   He has his
own positive opinion on all matters; not an unwise one,
usually, for his own ends; and will ask no advice of
yours.   He has no work to do—no tyrannical instinct
to obey.   The earth-worm has his digging and digest-
ing; the bee her gathering and building; the spider her
cunning net-work; the ant her treasury and accounts.
All things are comparatively slaves, or people of vulgar
business.   But your fly, free in the air, free in the
chamber—a black incarnation of caprice,—wandering,
investigating, flitting, flirting, feasting at his will, with
rich variety of choice in feast, from the heaped sweets in
the grocer's window to those of the butcher's back yard,
and from the galled place on your cab-horse's back, to
the brown spot in the road, from which, as the hoof
disturbs him, he rises with angry republican buzz—
what freedom is like his?

For captivity, again, perhaps your poor watch-dog
is as sorrowful a type as you will easily find.   Mine
certainly is.   The day is lovely, but I must write this,
and cannot go out with him.   He is chained in the
yard, because I do not like dogs in rooms, and the
gardener does not like dogs in gardens.   He has no
books,—nothing but his own weary thoughts for
company, and a group of those free flies, whom he snaps
at, with sullen ill success.   Such dim hope as he may

have that I may yet take him out with me, will be, hour by hour, disappointed, or worse, darkened at once into a leaden despair by an authoritative " No "—too well understood. His fidelity only seals his fate; (if he would not watch for me, he would be sent away, and go hunting with some happier master; but he watches, and is wise, and faithful, and miserable), and his high animal intellect only gives him the wistful power of wonder, and sorrow, and desire, and affection, which embitter his captivity. Yet of the two, would we rather be watch-dog or fly?

Indeed, the first point we have all to determine is not how free we are, but what kind of creatures we are. It is of small importance to any of us whether we get liberty; but of the greatest that we deserve it. Whether we can win it, fate must determine; but that we will be worthy of it, we may ourselves determine; and the sorrowfullest fate, of all that we can suffer, is to have it *without* deserving it.

I have hardly patience to hold my pen and go on writing, as I remember (I would that it were possible for a few consecutive instants to forget) the infinite follies of modern thought in this matter, centred in the notion that liberty is good for a man, irrespectively of the use he is likely to make of it. Folly unfathomable! unspeakable! unendurable to look in the full face of, as the laugh of a cretin. You will send your child, will you, into a room where the table is loaded with sweet wine and fruit—some poisoned, some not?— you will say to him, " Choose freely, my little child! It is so good for you to have freedom of choice: it forms your character—your individuality! If you take the wrong cup, or the wrong berry, you will die before the day is over, but you will have acquired the dignity of a Free child? "

You think that puts the case too sharply? I tell you, lover of liberty, there is no choice offered to you, but it is similarly between life and death. There is no act, nor option of act, possible, but the wrong deed or option has poison in it which will stay in your veins thereafter for ever.

Never more to all eternity can you be as you might have been, had you not done that—chosen that. You have " formed your character," forsooth! No; if you have chosen ill, you have De-formed it, and that for ever! In some choices, it had been better for you that a red hot iron bar had struck you aside, scarred and helpless, than that you had so chosen. " You will know better next time!" No. Next time will never come. Next time the choice will be in quite another aspect—between quite different things,—you, weaker than you were by the evil into which you have fallen; it, more doubtful than it was, by the increased dimness of your sight. No one ever gets wiser by doing wrong, nor stronger. You will get wiser and stronger only by doing right, whether forced or not; the prime, the one need is to do *that*, under whatever compulsion, till you can do it without compulsion. And then you are a Man.

" What!" a wayward youth might perhaps answer, incredulously; " no one ever gets wiser by doing wrong? Shall I not know the world best by trying the wrong of it, and repenting? Have I not, even as it is, learned much by many of my errors?" Indeed, the effort by which partially you recovered yourself was precious; that part of your thought by which you discerned the error was precious. What wisdom and strength you kept, and rightly used, are rewarded; and in the pain and the repentance, and in the acquaintance with the aspects of folly and sin, you have learned something; how much less than you would have learned in right paths, can never be told, but that it *is* less is certain. Your liberty of choice has simply destroyed for you so much life and strength, never regainable. It is true you now know the habits of swine, and the taste of husks: do you think your father could not have taught you to know better habits and pleasanter tastes, if you had stayed in his house; and that the knowledge you have lost would not have been more, as well as sweeter, than that you have gained? But " it so forms my individuality to be free! " Your individuality was given you by God, and in your race; and if you have any to speak of, you will want no liberty. You will want a den to work in, and peace, and light—no more, in absolute need; if more, in any wise, it will still not be liberty, but direction, instruction, reproof, and sympathy. But if you have no individuality, if there is no true character nor true desire in you, then you will indeed want to be free. You will begin early, and as a boy desire to be a man, and, as a man, think yourself as good as every other. You will choose freely to eat, freely to drink, freely to stagger and fall; freely, at last, to curse yourself and die. That is the only and final freedom possible to us; and that is consummate freedom,—permission for every particle in the rotting body to leave its neighbour particle, and shift for itself. You call it " corruption " in the flesh; but before it comes to that, all liberty is an equal corruption in mind. You ask for freedom of thought; but if you have not sufficient grounds for thought, you have no business to think; and if you have sufficient grounds, you have no business to think wrong. Only one thought is possible to you, if you are wise—your liberty is geometrically proportionate to your folly. " But all this glory and activity of our age! what are they owing to, but to our freedom of thought? " In a measure, they are owing—what good is in them—to the discovery of many lies, and the escape from the power of evil. Not to liberty, but to the deliverance from an evil or cruel master. Brave men have dared to examine lies which had long been taught, not because they were *free*-thinkers, but because they were such stern and close thinkers that the lie could no longer escape them. Of course the restriction of thought, or of its expression, by persecution, is merely a form of violence; justifiable or not, as other violence is, according to the character of the persons against whom it is exercised, and the divine and external laws which it vindicates, or violates. We must not burn a man alive for saying that the Athanasian creed is ungrammatical, nor stop a bishop's salary because we are getting the worst of an argument with him; neither must we let drunken men howl in the public streets at night. There is much that is true in the part of Mr. Mills' essay on Liberty which treats of freedom of thought; many important truths are there beautifully expressed, but many as important are omitted; and the balance, therefore, cannot be struck. The liberty of expression, with a great nation, would become like that in a well-educated company, in which there is indeed freedom of speech, but not of clamour; or like that in an orderly senate, in which men who deserve to be heard, are heard in due time, and under determined restrictions. The degree of liberty you can rightly grant to a number of men is commonly in the inverse ratio of their desire for it; and a general hush, or call to order, would be often very desirable in this England of ours. For the rest, of any good or evil extant, it is impossible to say what measure is owing to restraint, and what to licence, where the right is balanced between them. I was not a little provoked one day, a summer or two since, in Scotland, because the Duke of Athole hindered me from examining the gneissose junctions in Glen Tilt, at the hour convenient to me; but I saw them at last, and in quietness; and to the very restriction that annoyed me, owed, probably, the fact of their being in existence, instead of being blasted away by a mob-company; while the free paths and inlets of Loch Katrine and the Lake of Geneva are for ever trampled down and destroyed, not by one duke, but by tens of thousands of ignorant tyrants.

So a Dean and a Chapter may, perhaps, unjustifiably

hinder me from seeing a cathedral without paying twopence; but your free mob pulls spire and all down about my ears, and I can see it no more for ever. And even if I cannot get up to the granite junctions in the glen, the stream comes down from them pure to the Garry; but in Beddington Park I am stopped by the newly-erected fence of a building speculator, and the bright Wandel, divine of waters as Castaly, is filled by the free public with old shoes, obscene crockery, and ashes.

In fine, the arguments for liberty may in general be summed in a few very simple forms, as follows:—

1. Misguiding is mischievous; therefore guiding is.

2. If the blind lead the blind, both fall into the ditch: therefore, nobody should lead anybody.

3. Lambs and fawns should be left free in the fields; much more bears and wolves.

4. If a man's gun and bullets are his own, he may fire in any direction he pleases.

5. A fence across a road is inconvenient; much more one at the side of it.

6. Babes should not be swaddled with their hands bound down to their sides; therefore they should be thrown out to roll in the kennels, naked.

None of these arguments are good, and the practical issues of them are worse. For the fact is, that there are certain eternal laws for human conduct, which are quite clearly discernible by human reason. So far as they are discovered and obeyed, by whatever machinery or authority the obedience is procured, there follow life and strength. So far as they are disobeyed, by whatever machinery the disobedience is brought about, there follow impotence and dissolution. And the first duty of every man in the world is to find his true master, and submit to him; and to find his true inferior, and conquer him. The punishment is sure, if you either refuse the reverence, or are too cowardly and indolent to enforce the compulsion. A base nation crucifies or poisons its wise men, and lets its fools rave about the streets.   A wise nation obeys the one, restrains the other, and disciplines all.

The best examples of the results of wise normal discipline in Art will be found in whatever evidence remains respecting the lives of great Italian painters in eras of progress.   But just in proportion to the admirableness and efficiency of the life, will be usually the scantiness of its history.   The individualities and liberties which are only causes of destruction may be recorded, but the loyal conditions of its daily breath are never told. Because Leonardo made models of machines, dug canals, built fortifications, and dissipated half his Art-power in capricious ingenuities, we have many anecdotes of him, but no picture of importance on canvas, and only a few withered stains of one upon a wall.   But because his pupil, or reputed pupil, Luini, laboured in constant and successful simplicity, we have no anecdotes of him, though hundreds of noble works.   Luini is, perhaps, the best central type of the highly-trained Italian painter.   He is the only man who entirely unites the religious temper which was the spirit-life of Art, with the physical power which was its bodily life.   He joins the purity and passion of Angelico to the strength of Veronese; the two elements, poised in perfect balance, are so calmed and restrained each by the other, that most observers lose the sense of both.   The artist does not see his strength, because of the chastened spirit in which it is used, and the religious visionary does not recognise his passion, by reason of the frank human truth with which it is rendered.   He is a man ten times greater than Leonardo;—a mighty colourist, while Leonardo was only a fine draughtsman in black, staining the chiaroscuro drawing, like a coloured print.   He perceived and rendered the delicatest types of human beauty that have been painted since the days of the Greeks, while Leonardo polluted all his finer instincts by caricature, and remained to the end of his days the slave of an archaic smile; and he is a designer as frank, instinctive, and exhaustless as Tintoret, while Leonardo's design is only an agony of science, admired chiefly because it is painful, and capable of analysis in its best accomplishment.   Luini has left nothing behind him that is not lovely, or that is accusable in any definite error; but of his life I believe hardly anything is known beyond remnants of tradition which murmur about Lugano and Saronno, and which remain ungleaned. This only is certain, that he was born in the loveliest district of North Italy, where hills and streams and air meet in softest harmonies.   Child of the Alps, and of their divinest lake, he is taught, without doubt or dismay, a lofty religious creed, and a sufficient law of life, and of its mechanical arts.   Whether lessoned by Leonardo himself, or merely one of many disciplined in the system of the Milanese school, he learns unerringly to draw, unerringly and enduringly to paint.   His tasks are set him without question day by day, by men who are justly satisfied with his work, and who accept it without any harmful praise, or senseless blame.   Place, scale, and subject are determined for him on the cloister wall or the church dome; as he is required, for his suffi- cient daily bread, he paints what he has been taught to design wisely, and has passion to realise gloriously; every touch he lays is eternal, every thought he con- ceives is beautiful and pure; his hand moves always in radiance of blessing; from day to day his life enlarges in power and peace; it passes away cloudlessly, the starry twilight remaining yet, arched far against the night.

  Oppose to such a life as this that of a great painter amidst the elements of modern English liberty.   Take the life of Turner, in whom the artistic energy and inherent love of beauty were at least as strong as in Luini; but, amidst the disorder and ghastliness of the lower streets of London, his instincts in early infancy were warped into toleration of evil, or even delight in it.

He gathers what he can of instruction by questioning and prying among half-informed masters; spells out some knowledge of classical fable; educates and shapes himself, by an admirable force, to the production of wildly majestic, or pathetically tender and pure pictures, by which he cannot live.   There is no one to judge them, or to command him; only some of the English upper classes hire him to paint their houses and parks, and destroy the drawings afterwards by the most wanton neglect.   Tired of labouring carefully without either reward or praise, he dashes out into various experimental and popular works—makes himself the servant of the lower public, and is dragged hither and thither at their heels; while yet, helpless and guideless, he indulges his idiosyncrasies till they change into insanities; the nobleness and strength of his soul increasing its sufferings, and giving force to its errors; all the purpose and power of life degenerating into instinct; and the web of his work wrought at last of beauties too subtle to be understood, mixed with vices too singular to be forgiven—all useless, just because the magnificent idiosyncrasy had become one of solitude, or contention, in midst of a reckless populace, instead of submitting itself in loyal harmony to the Art-laws of an understanding nation.   And the life passed away in darkness and tears, and its work, in all the best beauty of it, has already perished, only enough remaining to teach us what we have lost.

These are the opposite effects of Law and of Liberty on men of the highest powers.   In the case of inferiors the contrast is still more fatal; under strict law, they become the subordinate workers in great schools, healthily aiding, echoing, or supplying with multitudinous force of hand, the mind of the leading masters: they are the nameless carvers of great architecture—stainers of glass—hammerers of iron—helpful scholars, whose work ranks round, if not with, their master's, and never disgraces it.   But the inferiors under a system of licence for the most part perish in miserable effort; a few struggle into pernicious eminence—harmful alike to themselves and to all who admire them; many die of starvation; many insane, either in weakness of insolent egotism, like Haydon, or in a conscientious agony of ignorant purpose and warped power, like Blake. There is no probability of the persistence of a licentious schoo! in any good accidentally discovered by them; there is an approximate certainty of their gathering with acclaim round any shadow of evil, and following it to whatever quarter of destruction it may lead.

It was in the full persuasion of these facts, and of the consequent necessity of some statement of law for our schools, that I began these papers, hoping they might fall chiefly into the form of discussion.

That in such a journal as this I should obtain no answer to so simple a question as the first I asked, respecting the proper character and use of the black outline, is itself a fact of some significance. For the present I am tired of writing without help; and having stated, as far as I know them, the higher laws which bear on this elementary question, I leave it to such issue as my good editor and his artist readers' care to bring it to, until January, when, if nothing hinder, I will again take it up where they leave it for me.

N

CHAPTER VII

In recommencing this series of papers, I may perhaps take permission briefly to remind the reader of the special purpose which my desultory way of writing, (of so vast a subject I find it impossible to write otherwise than desultorily), may cause him sometimes to lose sight of; the ascertainment, namely, of some laws for present practice of Art in our schools, which may be admitted, if not with absolute, at least with a sufficient consent, by leading artists.

There are indeed many principles on which different men must ever be at variance; others, respecting which it may be impossible to obtain any practical consent in certain phases of particular schools. But there are a few, which, I think, in all times of meritorious Art, the leading painters would admit; and others which, by discussion, might be arrived at, as, at all events, the best discoverable for the time.

One of those which I suppose great workmen would always admit, is, that, whatever material we use, the virtues of that material are to be exhibited, and its defects frankly admitted; no effort being made to conquer those defects by such skill as may make the material resemble another. For instance, in the dispute so frequently revived by the public, touching the relative merits of oil colour and water colour; I do not think a great painter would ever consider it a merit in a water colour to have the " force of oil." He would like it to have the peculiar delicacy, paleness, and transparency belonging specially to its own material. On the other hand, I think he would not like an oil

painting to have the deadness or paleness of a water
colour. He would like it to have the deep shadows,
and the rich glow, and crumbling and bossy touches
which are alone attainable in oil colour. And if he
painted in fresco, he would neither aim at the transparency of water colour, nor the richness of oil; but
at luminous bloom of surface, and dignity of clearly
visible form. I do not think that this principle would
be disputed by artists of great power at any time, or
in any country; though, if by mischance they had
been compelled to work in one material, while desiring
the qualities only attainable in another, they might
strive, and meritoriously strive, for those better results,
with what they had under their hand. The change of
manner in William Hunt's work, in the later part of
his life, was an example of this. As his art became
more developed, he perceived in his subjects qualities
which it was impossible to express in the transparent
medium; and employed opaque white to draw with,
when the finer forms of relieved light could not be
otherwise followed. It was out of his power to do
more than this, since in later life any attempt to learn
the manipulation of oil colour would have been un-
advisable; and he obtained results of singular beauty;
though their preciousness and completion would never,
in a well-founded school of Art, have been trusted to
the frail substance of water colour.

But although I do not suppose that the abstract
principle of doing with each material what it is best
fitted to do, would be, in terms, anywhere denied; the
practical question is always, not what should be done
with this, or that, if everything were in our power;
but what can be, or ought to be, accomplished with the
means at our disposal, and in the circumstances under
which we must necessarily work. Thus, in the question
immediately before us, of the proper use of the black
line—it is easy to establish the proper virtue of Line
work, as essentially " De-Lineation," the expressing

by outline the true limits of forms, which distinguish and part them from other forms; just as the virtue of brush work is essentially breadth, softness, and blend-ing of forms. And, in the abstract, the point ought not to be used where the aim is not that of definition, nor the brush to be used where the aim is not that of breadth. Every painting in which the aim is primarily that of drawing, and every drawing in which the aim is primarily that of painting, must alike be in a measure erroneous. But it is one thing to determine what should be done with a black line, in a period of highly dis-ciplined and widely practised art, and quite another thing to say what should be done with it, at this present time, in England. Especially, the increasing interest and usefulness of our illustrated books render this an enquiry of very great social and educational importance. On the one side, the skill and felicity of the work spent upon them, and the advantage which young readers, if not those of all ages, *might* derive from having examples of good drawing put familiarly before their eyes, cannot be overrated; yet, on the other side, neither the admirable skill nor free felicity of the work can ultimately be held a counterpoise for the want— if there be a want—of sterling excellence: while, farther, this increased power of obtaining examples of art for private possession, at an almost nominal price, has two accompanying evils: it prevents the proper use of what we have, by dividing the attention, and continually leading us restlessly to demand new subjects of interest, while the old are as yet not half exhausted; and it prevents us—satisfied with the multiplication of minor art in our own possession— from looking for a better satisfaction in great public works.

Observe, first, it prevents the proper use of what we have. I often endeavour, though with little success, to conceive what would have been the effect on my mind, when I was a boy, of having such a book

given me as Watson's *Illustrated Robinson Crusoe.*" [1]
The edition I had was a small octavo one, in two
volumes, printed at the *Chiswick Press* in 1812. It
has, in each volume, eight or ten very rude vignettes,
about a couple of inches wide; cut in the simple,
but legitimate, manner of Bewick, and, though wholly
commonplace and devoid of beauty, yet, as far as they
go, rightly done; and here and there sufficiently suggestive of plain facts. I am quite unable to say how far
I wasted,—how far I spent to advantage,—the un-
countable hours during which I pored over these woodcuts; receiving more real sensation of sympathetic
terror from the drifting hair and fear-stricken face of
Crusoe dashed against the rock, in the rude attempt
at the representation of his escape from the wreck,
than I can now from the highest art; though the rocks
and water are alike cut only with a few twisted or
curved lines, and there is not the slightest attempt at
light and shade, or imitative resemblance. For one
thing, I am quite sure that being forced to make all I
could out of very little things; and to remain long
contented with them, not only in great part formed
the power of close analysis in my mind, and the habit
of steady contemplation; but rendered the power of
greater art over me, when I first saw it, as intense as
that of magic; so that it appealed to me like a vision
out of another world. On the other hand, this long
contentment with inferior work, and the consequent
acute enjoyment of whatever was the least suggestive
of truth in a higher degree, rendered me long careless
of the highest virtues of execution, and retarded, by
many years, the maturing and balancing of the general
power of judgment. And I am now, as I said, quite

[1] Routledge, 1864. The engraving is all by Dalziel. I do not
ask the reader's pardon for speaking of myself, with reference to
the point at issue. It is perhaps quite as modest to relate personal experience as to offer personal opinion; and the accurate
statement of such experience is, in questions of this sort, the only
contribution at present possible towards their solution.

unable to imagine what would have been the result upon me, of being enabled to study, instead of these coarse vignettes, such lovely and expressive work as that of Watson; suppose, for instance, the vignette at p. 87, which would have been sure to have caught my fancy, because of the dog, with its head on Crusoe's knee, looking up and trying to understand what is the matter with his master. It remains to be seen, and can only be known by experience, what will actually be the effect of these treasures on the minds of children that possess them. The result must be in some sort different from anything yet known; no such art was ever yet attainable by the youth of any nation. Yet of this there can, as I have just said, be no reasonable doubt;—that it is not well to make the imagination indolent, or take its work out of its hands by supplying continual pictures of what might be sufficiently con-ceived without pictures. Take, for instance, the pre-ceding vignette, in the same book, "Crusoe looking at the first shoots of barley." Nothing can be more natural or successful as a representation; but, after all, whatever the importance of the moment in Crusoe's history, the picture can show us nothing more than a man in a white shirt and dark pantaloons, in an attitude of surprise; and the imagination ought to be able to compass so much as this without help. And if so laborious aid be given, much more ought to be given. The virtue of Art, as of life, is that no line shall be in vain. Now the number of lines in this vignette, applied with full intention of thought in every touch, as they would have been by Holbein or Durer, are quite enough to have produced,—not a merely deceptive dash of local colour, with evanescent background,—but an entirely perfect piece of chiaroscuro, with its lights all truly limited and gradated, and with every form of leaf and rock in the background entirely right, complete, —and full, not of mere suggestion, but of accurate information, exactly such as the fancy by itself cannot furnish. A work so treated by any man of power and sentiment such as the designer of this vignette possesses, would be an eternal thing; ten in the volume, for real enduring and educational power, were worth two hundred in imperfect development, and would have been a perpetual possession to the reader; whereas one certain result of the multiplication of these lovely but imperfect drawings, is to increase the feverish thirst for excitement, and to weaken the power of attention by endless diversion and division. This volume, beautiful as it is, will be forgotten; the strength in it is, in final outcome, spent for nought; and others, and still others, following it, will " come like shadows, so depart."

There is, however, a quite different disadvantage, but no less grave, to be apprehended from this rich multiplication of private possession. The more we have of books, and cabinet pictures, and cabinet ornaments, and other such domestic objects of art, the less capable we shall become of understanding or enjoying the lofty character of work noble in scale, and intended for public service. The most practical and immediate distinction between the orders of " mean " and " high " Art, is that the first is private,—the second, public; the first for the individual,—the second for all. It may be that domestic Art is the only kind which is likely to flourish in a country of cold climate, and in the hands of a nation tempered as the English are; but it is necessary that we should at least understand the disadvantage under which we thus labour; and the duty of not allowing the untowardness of our circumstances, or the selfishness of our dispositions, to have unresisted and unchecked influence over the adopted style of our art. But this part of the subject requires to be examined at length, and I must therefore reserve it for the following paper.

CHAPTER VIII

In pursuing the question put at the close of the last paper, it must be observed that there are essentially two conditions under which we have to examine the difference between the effects of public and private Art on national prosperity. The first in immediate influence is their Economical function, the second their Ethical. We have first to consider what class of persons they in each case support; and, secondly, what classes they teach or please.

Looking over the list of the gift-books of this year, perhaps the first circumstance which would naturally strike us would be the number of persons living by this industry; and, in any consideration of the probable effects of a transference of the public attention to other kinds of work, we ought first to contemplate the result on the interests of the workman. The guinea spent on one of our ordinary illustrated gift-books is divided among—

1. A number of second-rate or third-rate artists, producing designs as fast as they can, and realising them up to the standard required by the public of that year. Men of consummate power may sometimes put their hands to the business; but exceptionally.
2. Engravers, trained to mechanical imitation of this second or third-rate work; of these engravers the inferior classes are usually much overworked.
3. Printers, paper-makers, ornamental binders, and other craftsmen.
4. Publishers and booksellers.

Let us suppose the book can be remuneratively
produced if there is a sale of five thousand copies.
Then £5000, contributed for it by the public, are
divided among the different workers;—it does not
matter what actual rate of division we assume, for the
mere object of comparison with other modes of em-
ploying the money; but let us say these £5000 are
divided among five hundred persons, giving on an
average £10 to each. And let us suppose these £10 to
be a fortnight's maintenance to each. Then, to maintain them through the year, twenty-five such books
must be published; or to keep certainly within the
mark of the probable cost of our autumnal gift-books,
suppose £100,000 are spent by the public, with resultant
supply of 100,000 households with one illustrated book,
of second or third-rate quality, each, (there being twenty
different books thus supplied,) and resultant maintenance of five hundred persons for the year, at severe
work of a second or third-rate order, mostly mechanical.

Now, if the mind of the nation, instead of private,
be set on public work, there is of course no expense
incurred for multiplication, or mechanical copying of
any kind, or for retail dealing. The £5000, instead
of being given for five thousand *copies* of the work,
and divided among five hundred persons, are given
for one original work, and given to one person. This
one person will of course employ assistants; but these
will be chosen by himself, and will form a superior class
of men, out of whom the future leading artists of the
time will rise in succession. The broad difference will
therefore be, that, in the one case, £5000 are divided
among five hundred persons of different classes, doing
second-rate or wholly mechanical work; and in the
other case, the same sum is divided among a few chosen
persons of the best material of mind producible by the
state, at the given epoch. It may seem an unfair
assumption that work for the public will be more
honestly and earnestly done than that for private

possession. But every motive that can touch either conscience or ambition is brought to bear upon the artist who is employed on a public service, and only a few such motives in other modes of occupation. The greater permanence, scale, dignity of office, and fuller display of Art in a National building, combine to call forth the energies of the artist; and if a man will not do his best under such circumstances, there is no " best " in him.

It might also at first seem an unwarrantable assumption that fewer persons would be employed in the private than in the national work, since, at least in architecture, quite as many subordinate craftsmen are employed as in the production of a book. It is, however, necessary, for the purpose of clearly seeing the effect of the two forms of occupation, that we should oppose them where their contrast is most complete; and that we should compare, not merely bookbinding with brick-laying, but the presentation of Art in books, necessarily involving much subordinate employment, with its presentation in statues or wall-pictures, involving only the labour of the artist and of his immediate assistants. In the one case, then, I repeat, the sum set aside by the public for Art-purposes is divided among many persons very indiscriminately chosen; in the other, among few, carefully chosen. But it does not, for that reason, support fewer persons. The few artists live on their larger incomes,[1] by expenditure among various tradesmen, who in no wise produce Art, but the means of pleasant life; so that the real economical question is, not how many men shall we maintain, but at what work shall they be kept?—shall they every one be set to produce Art for us, in which case they must all live poorly, and produce bad Art; or out of

---

[1] It may be, they would not ask larger incomes in a time of highest national life; and that then the noble art would be far cheaper to the nation than the ignoble. But I speak of existing circumstances.

the whole number shall ten be chosen who can and will produce noble Art; and shall the others be employed in providing the means of pleasant life for these chosen ten? Will you have, that is to say, four hundred and ninety tradesmen, butchers, carpet-weavers, carpenters, and the like, and ten fine artists, or will you, under the vain hope of finding, for each of them within your realm "five hundred good as he," have your full complement of bad draughtsmen, and retail distributors of their bad work?

It will be seen in a moment that this is no question of economy merely; but, as all economical questions become, when set on their true foundation, a dilemma relating to modes of discipline and education. It is only one instance of the perpetually recurring offer to our choice—shall we have one man educated perfectly, and others trained only to serve him, or shall we have all educated equally ill?—Which, when the outcries of mere tyranny and pride-defiant on one side, and of mere envy and pride-concupiscent on the other, excited by the peril and promise of a changeful time, shall be a little abated, will be found to be, in brief terms, the one social question of the day.

Without attempting an answer which would lead us far from the business in hand, I pass to the Ethical part of the enquiry; to examine, namely, the effect of this cheaply diffused Art on the public mind.

The first great principle we have to hold by in dealing with the matter is, that the end of Art is NOT to *amuse;* and that all Art which proposes amusement as its end, or which is sought for that end, must be of an inferior, and is probably of a harmful, class.

The end of Art is as serious as that of all other beautiful things—of the blue sky and the green grass, and the clouds and the dew. They are either useless, or they are of much deeper function than giving amusement. Whatever delight we take in them, be it less or more, is not the delight we take in play, or receive from momentary surprise. It might be a matter of some metaphysical difficulty to define the two kinds of pleasure, but it is perfectly easy for any of us to feel that there *is* generic difference between the delight we have in seeing a comedy, and in watching a sunrise. Not but that there is a kind of Divina Commedia,—a dramatic change and power,—in all beautiful things: the joy of surprise and incident mingles in music, painting, architecture, and natural beauty itself, in an ennobled and enduring manner, with the perfectness of eternal hue and form. But whenever the desire of change becomes principal; whenever we care only for new tunes, and new pictures, and new scenes, all power of enjoying Nature or Art is so far perished from us; and a child's love of toys has taken its place. The continual advertisement of new music (as if novelty were its virtue) signifies, in the inner fact of it, that no one now cares for music. The continual desire for new exhibitions means that we do not care for pictures; the continual demand for new books means that nobody cares to read.

Not that it would necessarily, and at all times, mean this; for in a living school of Art there will always be an exceeding thirst for, and eager watching of, freshly-developed thought. But it specially and sternly means this, when the interest is merely in the novelty; and great work in our possession is forgotten, while mean work, because strange and of some personal interest, is annually made the subject of eager observation and discussion. As long as (for one of many instances of such neglect) two great pictures of Tintoret's lie rolled up in an outhouse at Venice, all the exhibitions and schools in Europe mean nothing but promotion of costly commerce. Through that, we might indeed arrive at better things; but there is no proof, in the eager talk of the public about Art, that we *are* arriving at them. Portraiture of the said public's many faces, and tickling of its twice as many eyes, by changeful phantasm,

are all that the patron-multitudes of the present day
in reality seek; and this may be supplied to them in
multiplying excess for ever, yet no steps made to the
formation of a school of Art now, or to the understanding of any that have hitherto existed.

It is the carrying of this annual Exhibition into the
recesses of home which is especially to be dreaded in
the multiplication of inferior Art for private possession.
Public amusement or excitement may often be quite
wholesomely sought, in gay spectacles or enthusiastic
festivals; but we must be careful to the uttermost how
we allow the desire for any kind of excitement to mingle
among the peaceful continuities of home happiness.
The one stern condition of that happiness is, that our
possessions should be no more than we can thoroughly
use; and that to this use they should be practically
and continually put.   Calculate the hours which, during
the possible duration of life, can, under the most favour-
able circumstances, be employed in reading, and the
number of books which it is possible to read in that
utmost space of time;—it will be soon seen what a limited
library is all that we need, and how careful we ought
to be in choosing its volumes.   Similarly, the time
which most people have at their command for any
observation of Art is not more than would be required
for the just understanding of the works of one great
master.   How are we to estimate the futility of wasting this fragment of time on works from which nothing
can be learned?   For the only real pleasure, and the
richest of all amusements, to be derived from either
reading or looking, are in the steady progress of the
mind and heart, which day by day are more deeply
satisfied, and yet more divinely athirst.

As far as I know the homes of England at the present
day, they show a grievous tendency to fall, in these
important respects, into the two great classes of over-
furnished and underfurnished:—of those in which the
Greek marble in its niche, and the precious shelf-loads

of the luxurious library, leave the inmates nevertheless
dependent for all their true pastime on horse, gun, and
croquet ground;—and those in which Art, honoured only
by the presence of a couple of engravings from Land-
seer, and literature, represented by a few magazines and
annuals arranged in a star on the drawing-room table,
are felt to be entirely foreign to the daily business of
life, and entirely unnecessary to its domestic pleasures.

The introduction of furniture of Art into households
of this latter class is now taking place rapidly; and, of
course, by the usual system of the ingenious English
practical mind, will take place under the general law
of supply and demand; that is to say, that whatever
a class of consumers, entirely unacquainted with the
different qualities of the article they are buying, choose
to ask for, will be duly supplied to them by the trade.
I observe that this beautiful system is gradually extending lower and lower in education; and that children,
like grown-up persons, are more and more able to obtain
their toys without any reference to what is useful or
useless, or right or wrong; but on the great horse-leech's
law of "demand and supply." And, indeed, I write
these papers, knowing well how effectless all speculations
on abstract proprieties or possibilities must be in the
present ravening state of national desire for excitement; but the tracing of moral or of mathematical
law brings its own quiet reward; though it may be, for
the time, impossible to apply either to use.

The power of the new influences which have been
brought to bear on the middle-class mind, with respect
to Art, may be sufficiently seen in the great rise in the
price of pictures, which has taken place (principally
during the last twenty years) owing to the interest
occasioned by national exhibitions, coupled with facilities of carriage, stimulating the activity of dealers,
and the collateral discovery by mercantile men that
pictures are not a bad investment.

The following copy of a document in my own posses-

sion, will give us a sufficiently accurate standard of
Art-price at the date of it:—

> "LONDON, *June 11th*, 1814.
>
> "Received of Mr. Cooke the sum of twenty-two
> pounds ten shillings for three drawings, viz., Lyme,
> Land's End, and Poole.
>
> £22 10*s*.   "J. M. W. TURNER."

It would be a very pleasant surprise to me if any *one* of
these three (southern coast) drawings, for which the
artist received seven guineas each (the odd nine shillings
being, I suppose, for the great resource of tale-tellers
about Turner—"coach-hire") were now offered to me
by any dealer for a hundred.   The rise is somewhat
greater in the instance of Turner than of any other
unpopular [1] artist; but it is at least three hundred per
cent. on all work by artists of established reputation,
whether the public can themselves see anything in it,
or not.   A certain quantity of intelligent interest mixes,
of course, with the mere fever of desire for novelty;
and the excellent book illustrations, which are the
special subjects of our enquiry, are peculiarly adapted
to meet this; for there are at least twenty people who
know a good engraving or woodcut, for one who knows
a good picture.   The best book illustrations fall into
three main classes: fine line engravings (always grave
in purpose), typically represented by Goodall's illustrations to Rogers's poems;—fine woodcuts, or etchings,
grave in purpose, such as those by Dalziel, from
Thomson and Gilbert;—and fine woodcuts, or etchings, for purpose of caricature, such as Leech's and
Tenniel's, in *Punch*.   Each of these have a possibly
instructive power special to them, which we will
endeavour severally to examine in the next chapter.

[1] I have never found more than two people (students excepted)
in the room occupied by Turner's drawings at Kensington, and
one of the two, if there *are* two, always looks as if he had got in
by mistake.

CHAPTER IX

I PURPOSE in this chapter, as intimated in the last, to sketch briefly what I believe to be the real uses and powers of the three kinds of engraving, by black line; either for book illustration, or general public instruction by distribution of multiplied copies. After thus stating what seems to me the proper purpose of each kind of work, I may, perhaps, be able to trace some advisable limitations of its technical methods.

I. And first, of pure line engraving.

This is the only means by which entire refinement of intellectual representation can be given to the public. Photographs have an inimitable mechanical refinement, and their legal evidence is of great use if you know how to cross-examine them. They are popularly supposed to be " true," and, at the worst, they are so, in the sense in which an echo is true to a conversation of which it omits the most important syllables and reduplicates the rest. But this truth of mere transcript has nothing to do with Art properly so called; and will never supersede it. Delicate art of design, or of selected truth, can only be presented to the general public by true line engraving. It will be enough for my purpose to instance three books in which its power has been sincerely used. I am more in fields than libraries, and have never cared to look much into book illustrations; there are, therefore, of course, numbers of well-illustrated works of which I know nothing: but the three I should myself name as typical of good use of the method, are I. Rogers's Poems, II. the Leipsic edition of Heyne's Virgil (1800), and, III. the great *Description de l'Egypte*.

The vignettes in the first-named volumes (considering

the Italy and Poems as one book) I believe to be as
skilful and tender as any hand work, of the kind, ever
done; they are also wholly free from affectation of
overwrought fineness, on the one side, and from hasty
or cheap expediencies on the other; and they were
produced under the direction and influence of a gentleman and a scholar.   Multitudes of works, imitative of
these, and far more attractive, have been produced
since; but none of any sterling quality: the good books
were (I was told) a loss to their publisher, and the money
spent since in the same manner has been wholly thrown
away.   Yet these volumes are enough to show what
lovely service line engraving might be put upon, if the
general taste were advanced enough to desire it.   Their
vignettes from Stothard, however conventional, show
in the grace and tenderness of their living subjects how
types of innocent beauty, as pure as Angelico's, and far
lovelier, might indeed be given from modern English
life, to exalt the conception of youthful dignity and
sweetness in every household.   I know nothing among
the phenomena of the present age more sorrowful than
that the beauty of our youth should remain wholly un-
represented in Fine Art, because unfelt by ourselves;
and that the only vestiges of a likeness to it should be
in some of the more subtle passages of caricatures,
popular (and justly popular) as much because they were
the only attainable reflection of the prettiness, as
because they were the only sympathising records of the
humours, of English girls and boys.   Of our oil portraits
of them, in which their beauty is always conceived as
consisting in a fixed simper—feet not more than two
inches long, and accessory grounds, pony, and groom—
our sentence need not be " *guarda e passa*," but " *passa* "
only.   Yet one oil picture has been painted, and, so far
as I know, one only, representing the deeper loveliness
of English youth—the portraits of the three children of
the Dean of Christ Church, by the son of the great
portrait painter, who has recorded whatever is tender

and beautiful in the faces of the aged men of England, bequeathing, as it seems, the beauty of their children to the genius of his child.

The second book which I named, Heyne's Virgil, shows, though unequally and insufficiently, what might be done by line engraving to give vital image of classical design, and symbol of classical thought. It is profoundly to be regretted that none of these old and well-illustrated classics can be put frankly into the hands of youth; while all books lately published for general service, pretending to classical illustration, are, in point of Art, absolutely dead and harmful rubbish. I cannot but think that the production of well-illustrated classics would at least leave free of money-scathe, and in great honour, any publisher who undertook it; and although school-boys in general might not care for any such help, to one, here and there, it would make all the difference between loving his work and hating it. For myself, I am quite certain that a single vignette like that of the fountain of Arethusa, in Heyne, would have set me on an eager quest, which would have saved me years of sluggish and fruitless labour.

It is the more strange, and the more to be regretted, that no such worthy applications of line engraving are now made, because, merely to gratify a fantastic pride, works are often undertaken in which, for want of well-educated draughtsmen, the mechanical skill of the engraver has been wholly wasted, and nothing produced useful, except for common reference. In the great work published by the Dilettanti Society, for instance, the engravers have been set to imitate, at endless cost of sickly fineness in dotted and hatched execution, drawings in which the light and shade is always forced and vulgar, if not utterly false. Constantly (as in the 37th plate of the first volume), waving hair casts a straight shadow, not only on the forehead, but even on the ripples of other curls emerging beneath it; while the publication of plate 41, as a representation of the most beautiful statue in the British Museum, may well arouse any artist's wonder what kind of " diletto " in antiquity it might be, from which the Society assumed its name.

The third book above-named as a typical example of right work in line, the *Description de l'Egypte*, is one of the greatest monuments of calm human industry, honestly and delicately applied, which exists in the world. The front of Rouen Cathedral, or the most richly-wrought illuminated missal, as pieces of resolute industry, are mere child's play compared to any group of the plates of natural history in this book. Of un-emotional, but devotedly earnest and rigidly faithful labour, I know no other such example. The lithographs to Agassiz's " poissons fossiles " are good in their kind, but it is a far lower and easier kind, and the popularly visible result is in larger proportion to the skill; whereas none but workmen can know the magnificent devotion of unpretending and observant toil, involved in even a single figure of an insect or a starfish on these un-approachable plates. Apply such skill to the simple presentation of the natural history of every English county, and make the books portable in size, and I cannot conceive any other book-gift to our youth so precious.

II. Wood-cutting and etching for serious purpose.

The tendency of wood-cutting in England has been to imitate the fineness and manner of engraving. This is a false tendency; and so far as the productions obtained under its influence have been successful, they are to be considered only as an inferior kind of engraving, under the last head. But the real power of wood-cutting is, with little labour, to express in clear delineation the most impressive essential qualities of form and light and shade, in objects which owe their interest not to grace, but to power and character. It can never express beauty of the subtlest kind, and is not in any way available on a large scale; but used rightly, on its own ground, it is the *most purely intellectual* of all Art; sculpture, even of the highest order, being slightly sensual and imitative; while fine wood-cutting is entirely abstract, thoughtful, and passionate. The best woodcuts that I know in the whole range of Art are those of Durer's *Life of the Virgin;* after these come the other works of Durer, slightly inferior from a more complex and wiry treatment of line. I have never seen any other work in wood deserving to be named with his; but the best vignettes of Bewick approach Durer in execution of plumage, as nearly as a clown's work can approach a gentleman's. Some very brilliant execution on an inferior system—less false, however, than the modern English one—has been exhibited by the French; and if we accept its false conditions, nothing can surpass the cleverness of our own school of Dalziel, or even of the average wood-cutting in our daily journals, which however, as aforesaid, is only to be reckoned an inferior method of engraving. These meet the demand of the imperfectly-educated public in every kind; and it would be absurd to urge any change in the method, as long as the public remain in the same stage of knowledge or temper. But, allowing for the time during which these illustrated papers have now been bringing whatever information and example of Art they could, to the million, it seems likely that the said million will remain in the same stage of knowledge yet for some time. Perhaps the horse is an animal as antagonistic to Art in England, as he was in harmony with it in Greece; still, allowing for the general intelligence of the London-bred lower clases, I was surprised by a paragraph in the *Pall Mall Gazette,* quoting the *Star* of November 6th of last year (1865), in its report upon the use made of illustrated papers by the omnibus stablemen to,—the following effect:—

" They are frequently employed in the omnibus-yards from five o'clock in the morning till twelve at night, so that a fair day's work for a ' horse-keeper ' is about

eighteen hours.   For this enormous labour they receive
a guinea per week, which for them means seven, not six,
days; though they do contrive to make Sunday an
' off-day ' now and then.   The ignorance of aught in the
world save ' 'orses and 'buses ' which prevails amongst
these stablemen is almost incredible.   A veteran horse-
keeper, who had passed his days in an omnibus-
yard, was once overheard praising the '*Lus-trated
London News* with much enthusiasm, as the best
periodical in London, ' leastways at the coffee-shop.'
When pressed for the reason of his partiality, he con-
fessed it was the ' pickshers ' which delighted him.
He amused himself during his meal-times by ' counting
the images! ' "

But for the classes among whom there is a real demand for educational art, it is highly singular that no
systematic use has yet been made of wood-cutting on
its own terms; and only here and there, even in the best
books, is there an example of what might be done by it.
The frontispieces to the two volumes of Mr. Birch's
Ancient Pottery and Porcelain, and such simpler cuts
as that at p. 273 of the first volume, show what might
be cheaply done for illustration of archaic classical
work; two or three volumes of such cuts chosen from
the best vases of European collections and illustrated
by a short and trustworthy commentary, would be to
any earnest schoolboy worth a whole library of common
books.   But his father can give him nothing of the kind
—and if the father himself wish to study Greek Art, he
must spend something like a hundred pounds to put
himself in possession of any sufficiently illustrative
books of reference.   As to any use of such· means for
representing objects in the round, the plate of the head
of Pallas facing p. 168 in the same volume sufficiently
shows the hopelessness of setting the modern engraver
to such service.   Again, in a book like Smith's diction-
ary of geography, the woodcuts of coins are at present
useful only for comparison and reference.   They are

absolutely valueless as representations of the art of the coin.

Now, supposing that an educated scholar and draughtsman had drawn each of these blocks, and that they had been cut with as much average skill as that employed in the woodcuts of *Punch*, each of these vignettes of coins might have been an exquisite lesson, both of high Art treatment in the coin, and of beautiful black and white drawing in the representation; and this just as cheaply—nay, more cheaply—than the present common and useless drawing. The things necessary are indeed not small,—nothing less than well-educated intellect and feeling in the draughtsmen; but intellect and feeling, as I have often said before now, are always to be had cheap if you go the right way about it—and they cannot otherwise be had for any price. There are quite brains enough, and there is quite sentiment enough, among the gentlemen of England to answer all the purposes of England: but if you so train your youths of the richer classes that they shall think it more gentlemanly to scrawl a figure on a bit of note paper, to be presently rolled up to light a cigar with, than to draw one nobly and rightly for the seeing of all men;—and if you practically show your youths, of all classes, that they will be held gentlemen, for babbling with a simper in Sunday pulpits; or grinning through, not a horse's, but a hound's, collar, in Saturday journals; or dirtily living on the public money in government non-offices:— but that they shall be held less than gentlemen for doing a man's work honestly with a man's right hand—you will of course find that intellect and feeling cannot be had when you want them. But if you like to train some of your best youth into scholarly artists,—men of the temper of Leonardo, of Holbein, of Durer, or of Velasquez, instead of decomposing them into the early efflorescences and putrescences of idle clerks, sharp lawyers, soft curates, and rotten journalists,—you will find that you can always get a good line drawn when you need it, without paying large subscriptions to schools of Art.

III. This relation of social character to the possible supply of good Art is still more direct when we include in our survey the mass of illustration coming under the general head of dramatic caricature, caricature that is to say, involving right understanding of the true grotesque in human life; caricature of which the worth or harmfulness cannot be estimated, unless we can first somewhat answer the wide question, What is the meaning and worth of English laughter? I say, " of English laughter," because if you can well determine the value of that, you determine the value of the true laughter of all men—the English laugh being the purest and truest in the metal that can be minted. And indeed only Heaven can know what the country owes to it, on the lips of such men as Sydney Smith and Thomas Hood. For indeed the true wit of all countries, but especially English wit (because the openest), must always be essentially on the side of truth—for the nature of wit is one with truth. Sentiment may be false—reasoning false — reverence false — love false, — everything false except wit; that *must* be true—and even if it is ever harmful, it is as divided against itself—a small truth undermining a mightier.

On the other hand, the spirit of levity, and habit of mockery, are among the chief instruments of final ruin both to individual and nations. I believe no business will ever be rightly done by a laughing Parliament; and that the public perception of vice or of folly which only finds expression in caricature, neither reforms the one, nor instructs the other. No man is fit for much, we know, " who has not a good laugh in him "—but a sad wise valour is the only complexion for a leader; and if there was ever a time for laughing in this dark and hollow world, I do not think it is now. This is a wide subject, and I must follow it in another place; for our present purpose, all that needs to be noted is that, for the expression of true humour, few and imperfect lines are often sufficient, and that in this direction lies the only opening for the serviceable presentation of amateur work to public notice.

I have said nothing of lithography, because, with the exception of Samuel Prout's sketches, no work of standard Art-value has ever been produced by it, nor can be: its opaque and gritty texture being wholly offensive to the eye of any well-trained artist. Its use in connection with colour is, of course, foreign to our present subject. Nor do I take any note of the various current patents for cheap modes of drawing, though they are sometimes to be thanked for rendering possible the publication of sketches like those of the pretty little "Voyage en Zigzag" ("how we spent the summer") published by Longman—which are full of charming humour, character, and freshness of expression; and might have lost more by the reduction to the severe terms of wood-cutting than they do by the ragged interruptions of line which are an inevitable defect in nearly all these cheap processes. It will be enough, therefore, for all serious purpose, that we confine ourselves to the study of the black line, as produced in steel and wood; and I will endeavour in the next paper to set down some of the technical laws belonging to each mode of its employment.

THE TEMPLE PRESS, PRINTERS, LETCHWORTH